Linear Earthwork, Tribal Boundary and Ritual Beheading: Aves Ditch from the Iron Age to the Early Middle Ages

Eberhard W. Sauer

with contributions by

Paul Booth, Patrick Erwin, Peter Hacking, Birgitta Hoffmann, Stephanie Knight and Mark Robinson

BAR British Series 402
2005

Published in 2016 by
BAR Publishing, Oxford

BAR British Series 402

Linear Earthwork, Tribal Boundary and Ritual Beheading:
Aves Ditch from the Iron Age to the Early Middle Ages

ISBN 978 1 84171 899 6

COVER IMAGE *(fig. 1): Aerial photograph of Aves Ditch: its southern end is visible as a linear cropmark running across the fields in the foreground, in the middle ground it is followed by a road and then a track, and a tree line marks its course in the background. NMR SP 5021/1= LN69 original number of Cambridge University of 26 April 1953 (oblique F24 Pan), held at Cambridge University Collection of Air Photographs, Unit for Landscape Modelling.*

BAR Publishing is the trading name of British Archaeological Reports (Oxford) Ltd.
British Archaeological Reports was first incorporated in 1974 to publish the BAR
Series, International and British. In 1992 Hadrian Books Ltd became part of the BAR
group. This volume was originally published by Archaeopress in conjunction with
British Archaeological Reports (Oxford) Ltd / Hadrian Books Ltd, the Series principal
publisher, in 2005. This present volume is published by BAR Publishing, 2016.

Printed in England

BAR
PUBLISHING

BAR titles are available from:

BAR Publishing
122 Banbury Rd, Oxford, OX2 7BP, UK
EMAIL   info@barpublishing.com
PHONE   +44 (0)1865 310431
FAX   +44 (0)1865 316916
www.barpublishing.com

TABLE OF CONTENTS

LIST OF ILLUSTRATIONS

Figures

Tables

INTRODUCTION

Aves Ditch is one of the best-preserved and yet most enigmatic of the ancient monuments in Oxfordshire, and it has remained a landmark to the present day. Lined by a straight row of trees (**figs 2 and 3**), it can be seen over a fair distance. It runs virtually dead straight (cf. Sauer 1998: 74) over no less than 4.2 km from north of Kirtlington to the modern parish boundary between Upper Heyford and Middleton Stoney (which, interestingly, follows its course). Remains of what may be its northern continuation, which does not follow the same straight alignment, can be traced to the vicinity of modern Fritwell (**fig. 4**).

Figure 2. Aves Ditch south-east of Caulcott, looking SSW on 16 December 1998: a parish boundary lined by trees and followed by a right of way.

Figure 3. Aves Ditch north of Goldwell Spinney looking NNE on 16 December 1998.

1

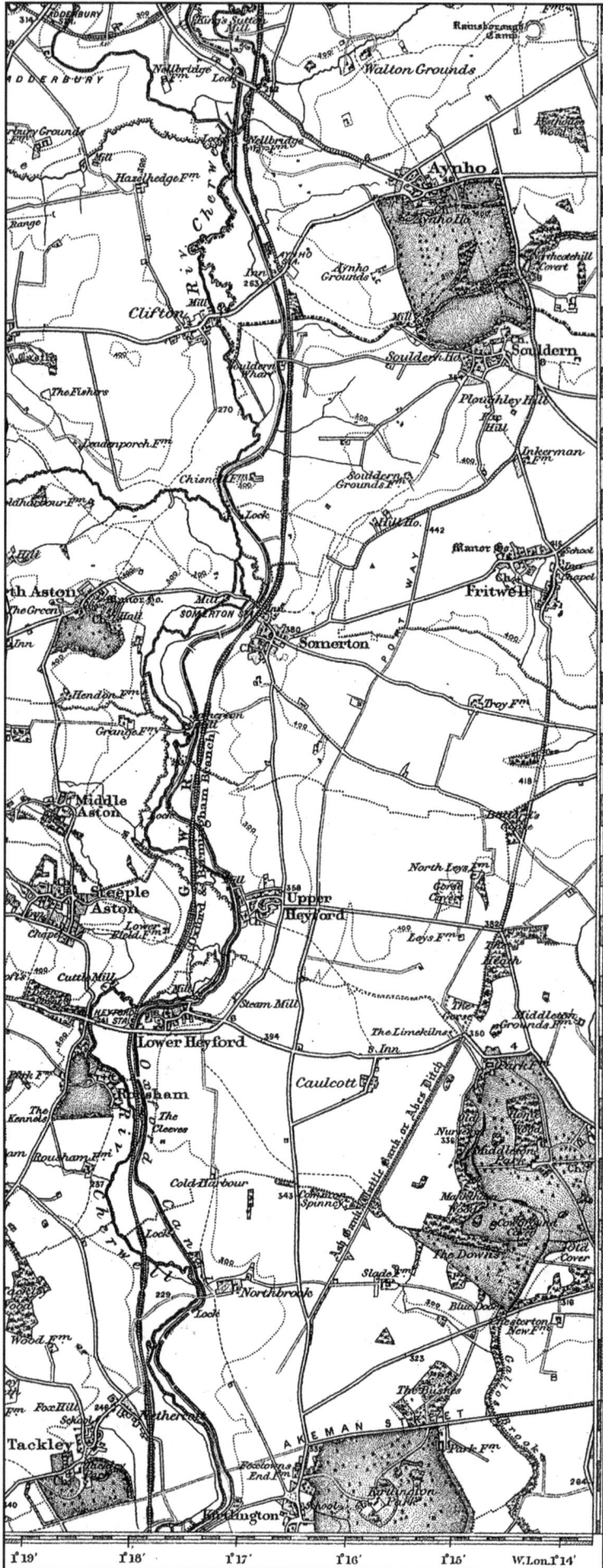

Figure 4. Extract of the 1 : 63,360 Ordnance Survey map, sheet 218 of 1890 with the entire extent of the earthwork; no continuation of the earthwork beyond a point just south of Fritwell could be found nor any obvious destination. Rainsborough Camp hillfort was no longer occupied in the late Iron Age and the early Roman period (Avery *et al.* 1968: esp. 292).

For over three centuries scholars have wondered whether it is of pre-Roman, Roman or Anglo-Saxon origin, whether it was a road or a linear earthwork and, in the latter case, what function it may have served. Notwithstanding this centuries-old debate and it being easily accessible just 15 to 22 km north of Oxford, it is also one of the least known of the county's visible archaeological features and is seldom referred to in popular or scholarly work on the history or archaeology of the region. Previously unpublished excavations of the 1930s and further work in the 1990s have contributed much to solving this enigma, and the present book provides the final report on these excavations.

Yet, the purpose of this monograph is not just to provide a description of six trenches, three each, excavated in 1937 and, 60 years later, in 1997/98. It also aims to investigate some of the key phenomena illuminated by these archaeological investigations, in a much wider context. These phenomena include the extent to which linear earthworks in various parts of the ancient world may have been positioned in boundary territory between different political or tribal communities, and for what practical and symbolic reasons so much effort was expended to build such monuments at the borders to other tribes or states. Directly linked to this set of questions is the evolution of such systems to mark or control boundaries. Is it possible, for example, to establish where (if anywhere) the prototype for Roman linear barriers, such as Hadrian's Wall, the Antonine Wall and the German 'Limes', has to be sought? It is appreciated that linear earthworks have a long tradition in European prehistory. However, prior to the introduction of tribal coinages or texts with relevant information, it is normally impossible to be certain whether or not the distribution zone of artefacts or distinctive forms of architecture bears any correlation to territories under some form of unified rule or government. Moreover, there is no other way to establish the extent of the latter. Thus, any study of the potential boundary function of prehistoric linear earthworks will in most instances involve a considerable element of uncertainty. In this survey, the phenomenon of linear earthworks at boundaries is therefore only explored in any detail for the period from the late Iron Age onwards.

A second phenomenon, however, expands the chronological range of topics explored from antiquity to the early Middle Ages. A decapitated skeleton of Anglo-Saxon date in Aves Ditch provides the opportunity to explore ritually beheaded skeletons in a much wider context. Superficially, it might seem that the phenomena of ancient linear earthworks and early medieval beheaded burials bear no relation to each other, other than, coincidentally, both being encountered in the same project. Yet, such an impression would not be true. I will argue that the placing of this mutilated burial in a linear ditch was by no means fortuitous. Quite the contrary, there are strong reasons to believe that Aves Ditch still functioned as a boundary in the Anglo-Saxon period, and that an unloved person was deliberately buried at the boundary. Far from being unrelated, the phenomena of linear earthworks and unusual burials allow us to make a strong case for a major monument having been associated by the local population with a powerful boundary feature for a minimum of 650 years. Aves Ditch thus provides evidence for long-term continuity in the ways an artificial landscape feature would have been looked at, and indeed parts of it still function as a parish boundary today.

SCOPE AND STRUCTURE OF THE FIELDWORK REPORT

To avoid duplication of information, no descriptive summary of the stratigraphy of individual trenches is provided here, but all relevant details are included in the discussion, the plans and sections, the list of contexts in tabular form (table 1) and the specialists' reports below. It is appreciated that some might have preferred a conventional 'objective' description of the 'facts' to be followed by a 'subjective' discussion. Yet, most descriptive summaries of observations contain an element of judgement; for example, even the attribution of what does, or does not, form part of a particular deposit (whose boundaries may not appear as sharp lines, but as gradual transition zones from one type of soil to the other) is not always as clear-cut as some archaeological manuals would have us believe. Rather than making any attempt to maintain the illusion that a separation between a section containing 100% fact and a section containing 100% interpretation is achievable, even if it was desirable, this excavation report has deliberately been written as an interpretative essay. Care has been taken to provide as much detail as possible and to make clear what the excavation team has, or believes it has observed and what were more subjective interpretations, yet without any attempt to subdivide the report into two polarised sections. The reader should find as much detail and as many clues to the level of objectivity and subjectivity of any statement as in a conventional excavation report, while the structure of the report is intended to sharpen our awareness that the transition between 'observation' and 'interpretation' is gradual and not bipolar.

Figure 5. Captain Christopher Musgrave, to whom we owe the first recorded excavations at Aves Ditch in 1937 and the accurate 3D-recording of the finds, in 1942 during the Second World War, in the Western Desert (cf. Roberts 2005: 20-1). Photo of the Ashmolean Museum, University of Oxford (Musgrave Archive), kindly provided by Sarah Parkin and Alison Roberts.

This report covers not only the 1997/98, but also the 1937 excavations, as far as the latter can be reconstructed from the concise published notes (Anon. 1937; 1938: 185; Harden 1939: 275-6) from a plan, the sections, finds and notes kept with them. The correspondence of the excavation director, Captain Christopher Musgrave (**fig. 5**), who died in 1978 (kindly made accessible by Alison Roberts of the Ashmolean Museum; cf. Musgrave Archive no. 4), contained little relevant information. No other written or photographic documentation of the 1937 fieldwork has been found, and an attempt to locate any surviving members of the team has equally been unsuccessful (information kindly supplied by Professor William Frend, president of the OUAS in Trinity Term 1936, letter of 2 February 2005). It seems likely that the Aves Ditch excavations were documented photographically, as Musgrave took a series of photographs on the excavations at the North Oxfordshire Grim's Ditch in 1935/36, some of which have been published (Harden 1937: pls VIIB-D, VIIIA-D, IXA and D, cf. 74). Hopefully, the relevant photographs and documents have not been destroyed and will come to light in future.

HISTORY OF RESEARCH

Aves Ditch is also known as Ash, Wattle, Goblins' or Arborough Bank and, in sections, as Soldiers', and Calcot Bank (Gelling 1953: 5; cf. 1979: 135; Plot 1677: 320; Rahtz and Rowley 1984: 5). In order to avoid confusion, the earthwork will be referred to as 'Aves Ditch' throughout this book and this term will be used for both elements of this linear installation, i.e. the ditch and the associated bank. In parts its bank and ditch are still well preserved, such as where we sectioned them in 1997/98, nowadays located within a wood with the telling name (Field 1993: 68) the 'Gorse' (**fig. 6**), but up to the earlier nineteenth century at the edge of the Heyford Heath (OSD 1814). In the late seventeenth century its good state of preservation in this area was noted by White Kennett (1695: 41), the vicar of Ambrosden, who attests that the bank, where it is cut by the road from Midlington (i.e. Middleton Stoney) to Heyford Bridge, is 'rising on each side to a considerable height'. Today the sections in immediate vicinity of the road, notably south of it, are badly preserved. The southernmost part of the earthwork, despite lying in an arable field, and being ploughed for a long period, is (contrary to Rahtz and Rowley 1984: 3) also still clearly visible, if the vegetation is low. With the exception of this arable section, a track and right of way follow most of the remainder of the earthwork. Between Mushroom Cottages and Goldwell Spinney (**fig. 7**) no remains are visible today, but the straight alignment of the track and the right of way suggest that it once followed this line and that its remains have been levelled by ploughing, rather than there being a gap. Aerial photographs offer support for this hypothesis, even if it cannot be excluded that we are seeing here secondary remains of a track rather than of the original earthwork. Within the 'Gorse' wood is the northern terminal of the straight section of the earthwork (**fig. 6**), but, after a gap, remains of a causeway, which may form the northern continuation of Aves Ditch, continue to a point near the southern outskirts of Fritwell (**fig. 8**).

Unsurprisingly, a feature, which so visibly dominates the landscape, already attracted the attention of antiquarian scholars. Yet, there was no agreement whether it dated to the Iron Age, the Roman or Saxon periods (though majority opinion originally tended towards the last of these three options), nor whether it functioned as a boundary, some other defensive earthwork, a road or a combination of more than one of these options. Plot (1677: 320-1), followed by Kennett (1695: 40-1, cf. 18, 32, glossary s.v. 'Aves Dich' [sic]) and Blomfield (1882: 25-7), considers the possibility that 'Aves' may derive from 'Offa's' and that it was, like Offa's Dyke, a Saxon boundary, although it could equally be a 'fore-fence of the Romans, raised against the Britans' (sic) '(or vice versa)' or, more likely still in his view, an ancient way. Similarly, Warton (1783: 48; cf. 69) thought that 'Avesditch or Offa's Ditch' was 'a partition between the Mercian and West-Saxon kingdoms' built soon after the late AD 770s when king

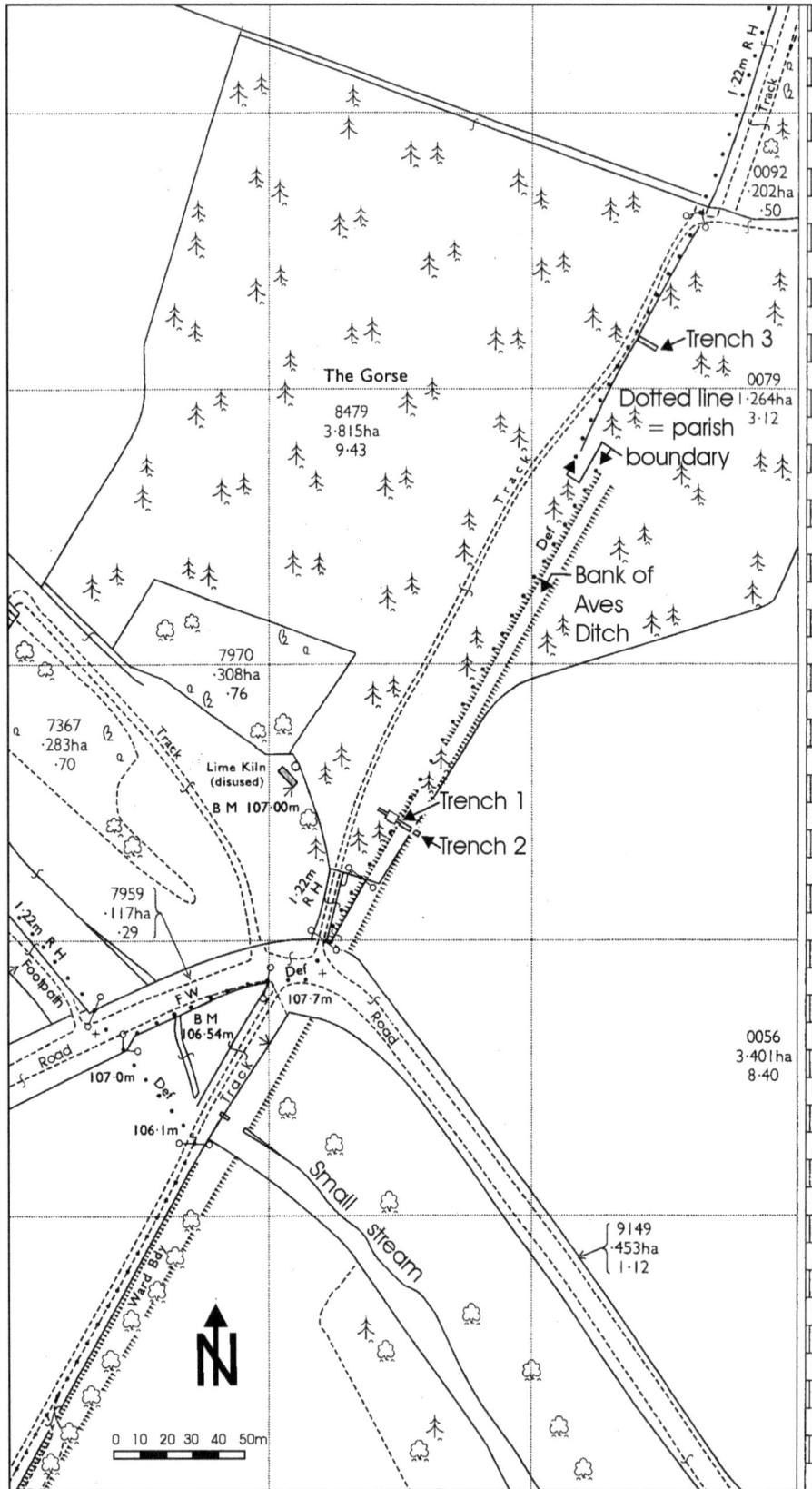

Figure 6. Location map of trenches 1, 2 and 3 in the Gorse. The northern terminal of the bank of Aves Ditch is NNE of trench 1, the crossroads c. 60 m SSE. An 18th-c. lime kiln and quarry are located to the north-west of trench 1. Reproduced from the 1 : 2,500 Ordnance Survey map, sheet SP 5024-5124, by kind permission of the Ordnance Survey. © Crown Copyright. NC/04/29585.

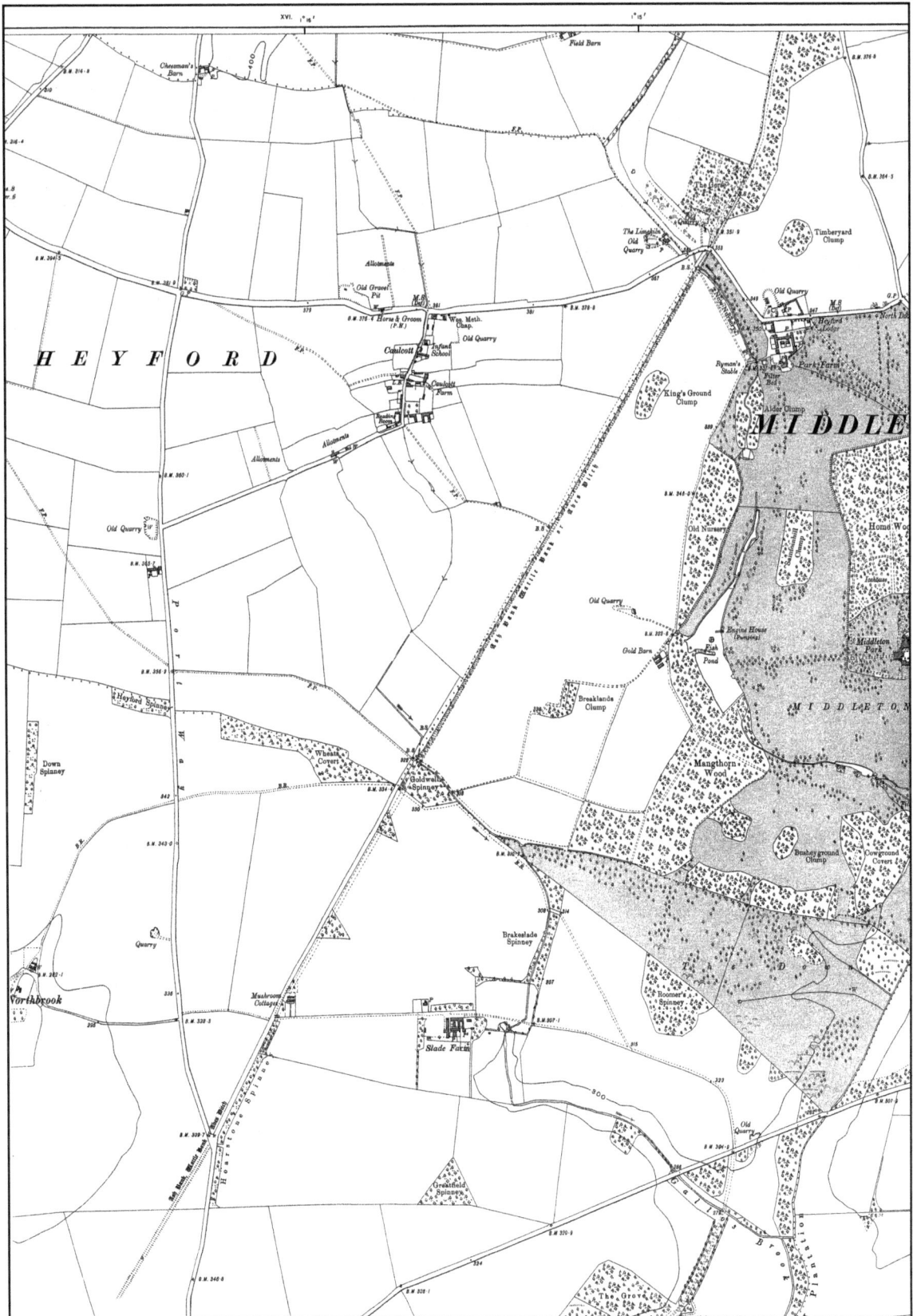

Figure 7. Extract of the 1 : 10560 Ordnance Survey map, Oxfordshire sheet XXII of 1923 showing the straight/ southern section of the earthwork. Scale reduced to 1 : 20,000.

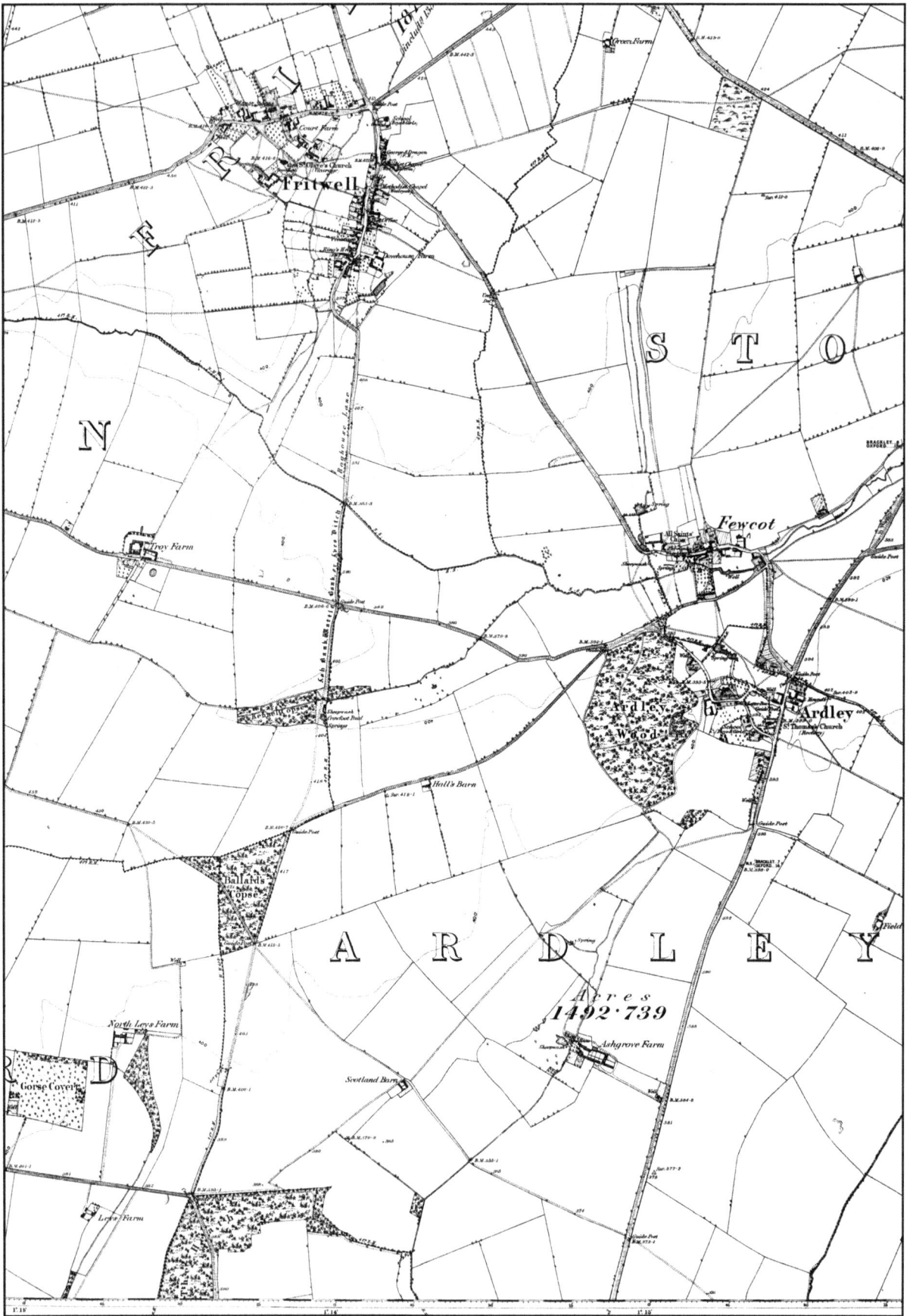

Figure 8. Extract of the 1 : 10560 Ordnance Survey map, Oxfordshire sheet XVI of 1885 (i.e. prior to the construction of the Upper Heyford Airfield) showing Chilgrove Drive (the lane from north of 'The Heath' to the now-destroyed Ballard's Copse) and Raghouse Lane, which may form a possible northern continuation of Aves Ditch. Scale reduced to 1 : 20,000. Reproduced by permission of the Trustees of the National Library of Scotland.

Offa had gained control over Oxfordshire. Beesley (1841: 38, cf. 29, 52, 56, pl. IV), sceptical about the attribution of the earthwork to king Offa, agrees with its military interpretation and thought that along this line there was 'an ancient way ... defended in some parts, on the east side, by the earthwork known as Avesditch, Wattlebank and Ashbank'. In 1929 O'Neil (1929: 31-3) postulated that Aves Ditch was a road on the basis of its orientation towards Tackley Ford.

These dating proposals and functional analyses were based on analogies, and intuition, as it was only in the 1930s that the first recorded excavation occurred. Grundy (Anon. note, Ordnance Survey Card SP 42 SE1, SMR Oxfordshire) is reported to have made a cutting through Aves Ditch at an unknown point and at an unknown date, without finding any traces of a Roman structure, and thus regarded it 'more as a tribal boundary'. Elsewhere he argued that it was followed by a Roman road (Grundy 1933b: 2, 109-10). In an undated pamphlet of around 1933 he postulated that for the most part the road runs on the dyke. He thought it possible that it was a Roman road, but very unlikely that it was a main road of any length. This appears to have been written before he sectioned it as the following sentence suggests: 'The question of its Roman origin could only be decided definitely by taking a section of it if there exist any part of it where modern road making has not destroyed its ancient character' (Grundy 1933a: 19, cf. 18). In March and April 1937 one trench was excavated at the southern terminal of the earthwork and two more sections through it further north by members of the Oxford University Archaeological Society (OUAS) under the direction of Captain Musgrave (**fig. 5**). (In order to differentiate them from trenches 1 to 3, excavated in 1997/98, they are referred to subsequently as numbers I, II and III.) Elsewhere (Anon. 1938: 185) the fieldwork is attributed to D.B. Harden. The two men had already worked together in the excavations at the North Oxfordshire Grim's Ditch in 1935 and 1936 (Harden 1937: 74), and Harden may well have been involved. However, Harden's own testimony and Musgrave's signature under the sheet with the plans and sections (Harden 1939: 276; cf. Musgrave Archive no. 4; manuscript drawings and correspondence in the Ashmolean Museum) suggest that it was Musgrave who took the leading role at Aves Ditch. The results of these excavations were published in six lines in *Oxoniensia* (Anon. 1937), where it was argued that 'Pottery found in the filling of the ditch and under the bank (which lay E. of the ditch) gave evidence that the earthwork is of Romano-British date'. An even briefer summary in the *Journal of Roman Studies* (Anon. 1938: 185) equally refers to 'evidence of its Roman date'. The fieldwork also yielded new insights into the extent and purpose of the monument: 'Trial-trenching at the S. end of the Ditch as marked on O.S. 6-inch Oxon. XXII SW.' (**fig. 7**) 'resulted in the discovery of a butt-end of the ditch almost exactly where it is marked on the map on the high ground E. of the river Cherwell' (Anon. 1937). The 'excavations ... have proved conclusively that this earthwork is a dyke, formed of a ditch and bank, and not a road at all' (Harden 1939: 276). This functional interpretation of the monument as an earthwork was adopted in the first volume of the *Victoria History of the County of Oxford*, by Harden (1939: 275-6), and in the sixth volume, although no decision is reached there whether it was a 'Romano-British earthwork' (Lobel 1959: 182) or an 'ancient pre-Roman dyke' (Lobel 1959: 7) or a 'pre-Saxon' monument (Lobel 1959: 219). In the *Buildings of England* it is classified as a Roman or later earthwork (Sherwood and Pevsner 1974: 678). Sebastian Rahtz and Trevor Rowley (1984: 3) equally argue for a Roman, perhaps late Roman date, on the basis of its straight alignment. Anthony Hands (1998: 11) points out that Aves Ditch broadly mirrors the Port Way (**fig. 4**) and is thus undecided whether or not both can be of Roman date.

Yet, despite excavations, not only the date, but also the functional analysis of the earthwork remained contentious. Several scholars were still convinced that it was a Roman road (e.g. Margary 1973: 159, 168 no. 161; Hargreaves *et al.* 1974; Wilson 1975; Chambers 1993: 46). There is indeed documentary evidence that much of it was used as a track in the late Middle Ages (Lobel 1959: 219) (and probably before), and there are still public footpaths and minor roads along most of Aves Ditch today, though this need not necessarily indicate that this was its primary, rather than a secondary, function.

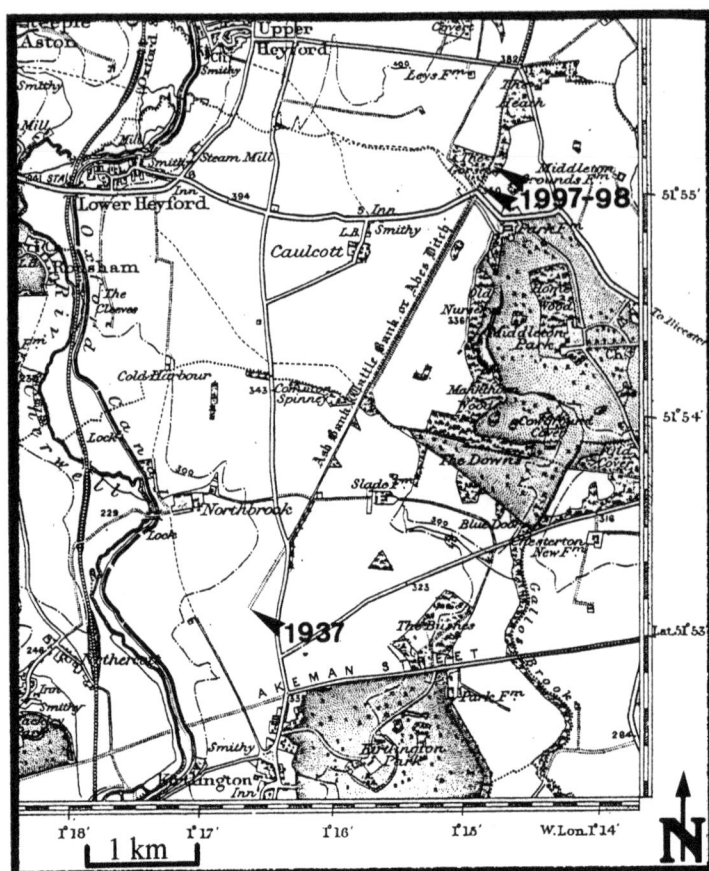

Figure 9. Location plan of the 1937 and 1997/98 trenches plotted
on the 1 : 63,360 Ordnance Survey map, sheet 218 of 1896.

It was to clarify the date and function of this enigmatic monument that the OUAS, who had also surveyed the postulated northern extension of the earthwork in 1946 (Atkinson 1946-1947), embarked upon another excavation, 60 years after the original project, in autumn 1997. We selected the Gorse for a several reasons: it contains one of the best-preserved sections of the monument, the wood allowed long-term access and, unlike most other sections, the public footpath was sufficiently far away from the earthwork to make its obstruction unnecessary (**fig. 6**). Furthermore, some distance from the 1937 trenches seemed preferable (**fig. 9**), to minimise the chances that any distorting factors (e.g. re-deposited material of similar origin) affected both excavations. The precise location of trench 1 within the well-preserved section was eventually determined by the fact that this was one of the few areas where no mature trees were in the way of a section through the monument at a right angle. Due to the depth of the stratigraphy, we reached in autumn 1997 neither the bottom of the ditch nor the natural bedrock under the bank. For this reason, and because of the unexpected discovery of a burial (see 'The beheaded skeleton' below), trench 1 was re-opened and extended in spring 1998 and two more trenches added (**figs 6 and 13**): no. 2 to find the east side of the bank and no. 3 to explore whether the straight section continued northwards of the point, up to which it is visible on the ground. The gap between trenches 1 and 2 was left in order to avoid having to cut down a section of a modern hedge (**figs 13 and 16, cf. 10 and 12**). Unfortunately, the back/ east side of the stone bank could not be located and must be precisely within this gap.

It ought to be stressed that the 1997/98 fieldwork was essentially confined to a highly targeted excavation carried out by students and other volunteers, mainly on weekends, on a very low budget. Neither the technical equipment nor the time or funding were available to conduct any topographical or geophysical surveys nor was there even time for field-walking. There is no doubt that employing these techniques would have allowed us to gain further insights and tie up the odd loose end, notably in relation to the enclosure to be discussed in the next section or the monument's southern terminal. Nevertheless, it was felt that the project had answered most of our questions (as far as material evidence had the potential to do so), and it seemed more important to publish our results than to try to resolve all outstanding questions, an attempt which undoubtedly would have thrown up at least as many additional questions as it would have answered.

THE IRON AGE ENCLOSURE PRE-DATING AVES DITCH AND OTHER SETTLEMENT IN THE VICINITY

Figure 10. The curving ditch underneath the bank in trench 1 looking ESE, 23 June 1998. Each segment of the scales (excl. the pointed tips) measures 500 mm.

The earliest feature encountered in our fieldwork 1997/98 was a curving ditch underlying the bank of Aves Ditch (**figs 10-13**). This ditch is probably associated with an irregular enclosure, visible on aerial photographs (**figs 14 and 15**; SP 5124/3-5, NMR 15119/09-10 & 14 and SP 5124/8-9 & 11, NMR 15112/25-6 & 29 of 12/7/1994), in the field immediately to the east the Gorse. There is a possible entrance in the southeast and, as in the case of Banjo enclosures, the access route leading to the entrance appears to be lined by a long ditch (on the north-east side); however, unlike a Banjo enclosure, no clear traces of a parallel ditch to form a funnel-shaped entrance are discernible on the opposite side. A series of banjo enclosures have been discovered to the north-east of this enclosure (e.g. SP 5224/4-6, NMR 15112/22-4 and SP 5225/1-3, NMR 15119/07-8 & 12 of 12/7/1994; SP 5226/18-20, NMR 21048/28-30 and SP 5226/21-2, NMR 21274/10-11 of 2/7/2001; SP 5227/1-3, NMR 15296/27-9 of 23/6/1995; SP 5227/4, NMR 15332/32 of 7/7/1995; SP 5227/29, NMR 18697/34 of 19/7/2000).

Figure 11. The curving ditch underneath the bank in trench 1 looking WNW, 23 June 1998. Each segment of the scales (excl. the pointed tips) measures 500 mm.

Figure 12. The curving ditch underneath the bank in trench 2 looking WNW, 5 July 1998. Each segment of the scales (excl. the pointed tips) measures 500 mm.

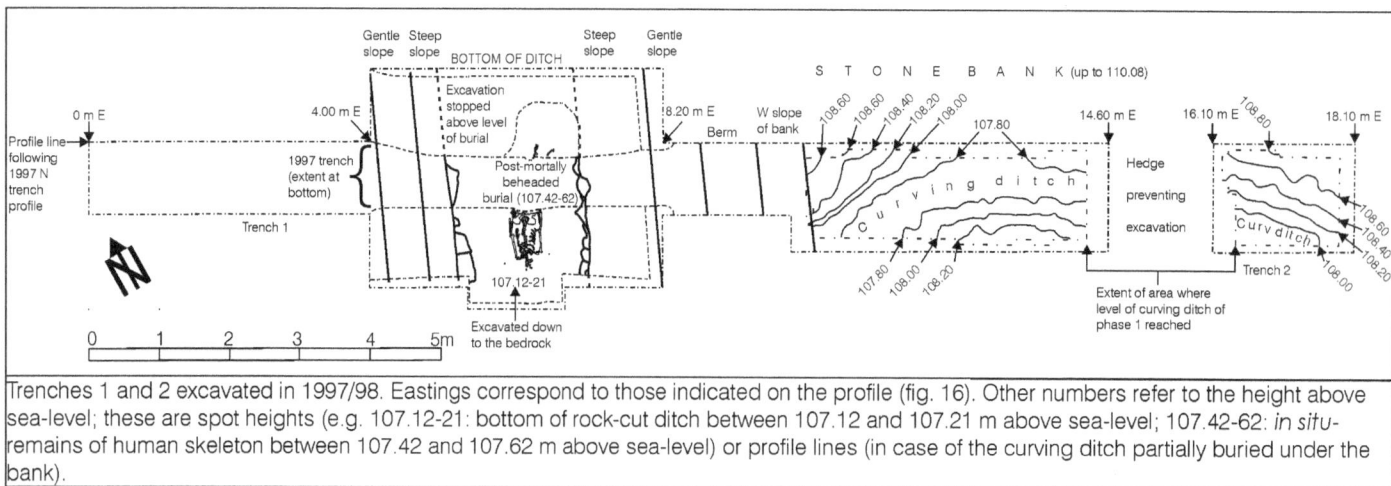

Trenches 1 and 2 excavated in 1997/98. Eastings correspond to those indicated on the profile (fig. 16). Other numbers refer to the height above sea-level; these are spot heights (e.g. 107.12-21: bottom of rock-cut ditch between 107.12 and 107.21 m above sea-level; 107.42-62: *in situ*-remains of human skeleton between 107.42 and 107.62 m above sea-level) or profile lines (in case of the curving ditch partially buried under the bank).

Figure 13. Plan of trenches 1 and 2.

Figure 14. Aerial photo of 12 July 1994. Trenches 1 and 2 of 1997/98 were 60 m north/ above the crossroads. Clearly visible is the enclosure in the field right/ east of the Gorse wood halfway between the crossroads and the point where the wood boundary turns at a c. 45 degree angle to the east. This enclosure is almost certainly associated with the curving ditch in trenches 1 and 2. Reproduced by kind permission of English Heritage. NMR 15119/09 (SP 5124/3). © Crown Copyright. NMR.

The aerial photographs suggest that the southern ditch of the enclosure runs into the present wood close to our trenches 1 and 2 (**fig. 14**), and it is thus likely that the curving ditch unearthed in our excavations is either the continuation of the southern enclosure ditch visible on the aerial photographs or, at least, associated with the enclosure. This ditched feature in the east of trench 1 and in trench 2 appears to curve away from the expected direction of the outer ditch around the south-western section of the enclosure. If it is part of the outer ditch, then this curvature would imply an irregular course. If not, it may form part of a different ditched feature, maybe associated with the enclosure. It is not possible to decide which is the more likely, as only a 7.50 m stretch of the ditch is known (including its likely course in the unexcavated gap between trenches 1 and 2), as the features visible on the aerial photographs have as yet not been plotted onto a map, and as no geophysical survey was carried out in the adjacent field. Such a survey immediately to the east of trenches 1 and 2 has the potential to clarify in future the relation (or, possibly, lack of relation) of our curving ditch to the enclosure.

Figure 15. Aerial photo of 12 July 1994 showing the crossroads and the wood in the Gorse above/ north of it. The straight tree-line from the right bottom corner to the crossroads follows Aves Ditch. Aves Ditch continues into the wood, but is not visible because of the tree cover. To the left/ west of Aves Ditch there are several enclosures. Another one is visible right/ east of the Gorse. Reproduced by kind permission of English Heritage. NMR 15119/14 (SP 5124/5). © Crown Copyright. NMR.

The high proportion of mid Iron Age pottery in trenches 1 and 2 (**fig. 16**) (as opposed to the predominance of late Iron Age pottery in the 1937 trenches I and II [**fig. 23**]), notably in the fill of the curving ditch (see Booth below), is likely to be a result of the re-deposition of material lost during a phase of intensive use of the enclosure. A high concentration of Iron Age pottery has also been observed in excavated Banjo enclosures, notably also in their enclosure ditches, in Micheldever (Hawkes 1987) and Wherwell (Brown 2000; Cunliffe and Poole 2000: 134) in Hampshire, despite the lack of evidence for permanent structures in the interior (Fasham 1987; Cunliffe and Poole 2000). Cunliffe and Poole (2000: 134-5) make the attractive suggestion that the enclosures were used for stock control, perhaps associated with communal feasting. This certainly could account for the high concentration of pottery (**fig. 16**) and animal bones, notably of sheep/ goat, but also of cattle, pigs and horses (see Knight below) in our curving ditch. Despite the lack of one antenna ditch, it is possible that the enclosure at Aves Ditch served a similar function. It is interesting to note that, according to Mark Robin-

— 110m W — 0 m E — t 1 — 4.60 m E

Section: ES; dating of pottery: PB.

! ? Iron Age pottery
⚲ Early/mid Iron Age
✦✧ Mid Iron Age
★ Later mid Iron Age
★☆ Late Iron Age (AD 1-50/70)
(Left: certain; right: ?)

Modern topsoil
Ancient topsoil

1, 20, 16, 7, 10

Aves Ditch in the Gorse (SP 5185 2465), 1997-1998
W = west, **E** = east, **t 1** = trench 1, **t 2** = trench 2
a = western section, **b** = central section, **c** = eastern section
1-32 = contexts 1-32 (not all contexts are represented in this profile; nos. 10, 11, 12, 16 and 32 [and 17?] are natural), **107 m/ 110 m** = height above sea-level

1 m

— 107m

a

! ? Roman pottery
⦿◎ Late 1st-2nd c. AD
◎ Late 1st-3rd c. AD
●○ Late 1st-4th c. AD
❷ 2nd c. AD
■ 2nd-4th c. AD
◆ AD 240-400

— 110 m — 11.40 m E

t 1

13, 15, 3, 18, 2, 16, 22, 10, 23

4.60 m E

Modern topsoil

Ancient topsoil

14, 17

Bottom of curving ditch projected onto the profile

6B, 6A, 10, 11, 8A, 8C, 8B, 9C, 11, 12, 12, 10

Archaeomagnetic samples

9A Limestone 9D bedrock 9B

Human burial with C14-date from right radius

— 107 m

b

11.40 m E — t 1 — **E 110m** — t 2 — 18.10 m E

1, 2, 4, 5A, 5B, 19, 3, 22, 23

24, 25, 29, 30, 31, 32

Stone bank
Location of back of bank
Deposits built up over curving ditch as a result of erosion
Top of rock-cut section of curving ditch
Bottom of curving ditch projected onto the profile

Soil, bank

Modern topsoil

Archaeomagnetic samples

C14-date from cattle metatarsal

Datable finds have been plotted onto the profile on the basis of their easting and the height above sea-level, irrespective of their distance to the profile. The centre of each symbol marks the actual findspot.

Other finds
⬟ Flint
⊞ C14-dated bones
Ⓡ Roman coin (AD 260-400)
Ⓒ Glass
♠ Post-medieval objects

107m

c

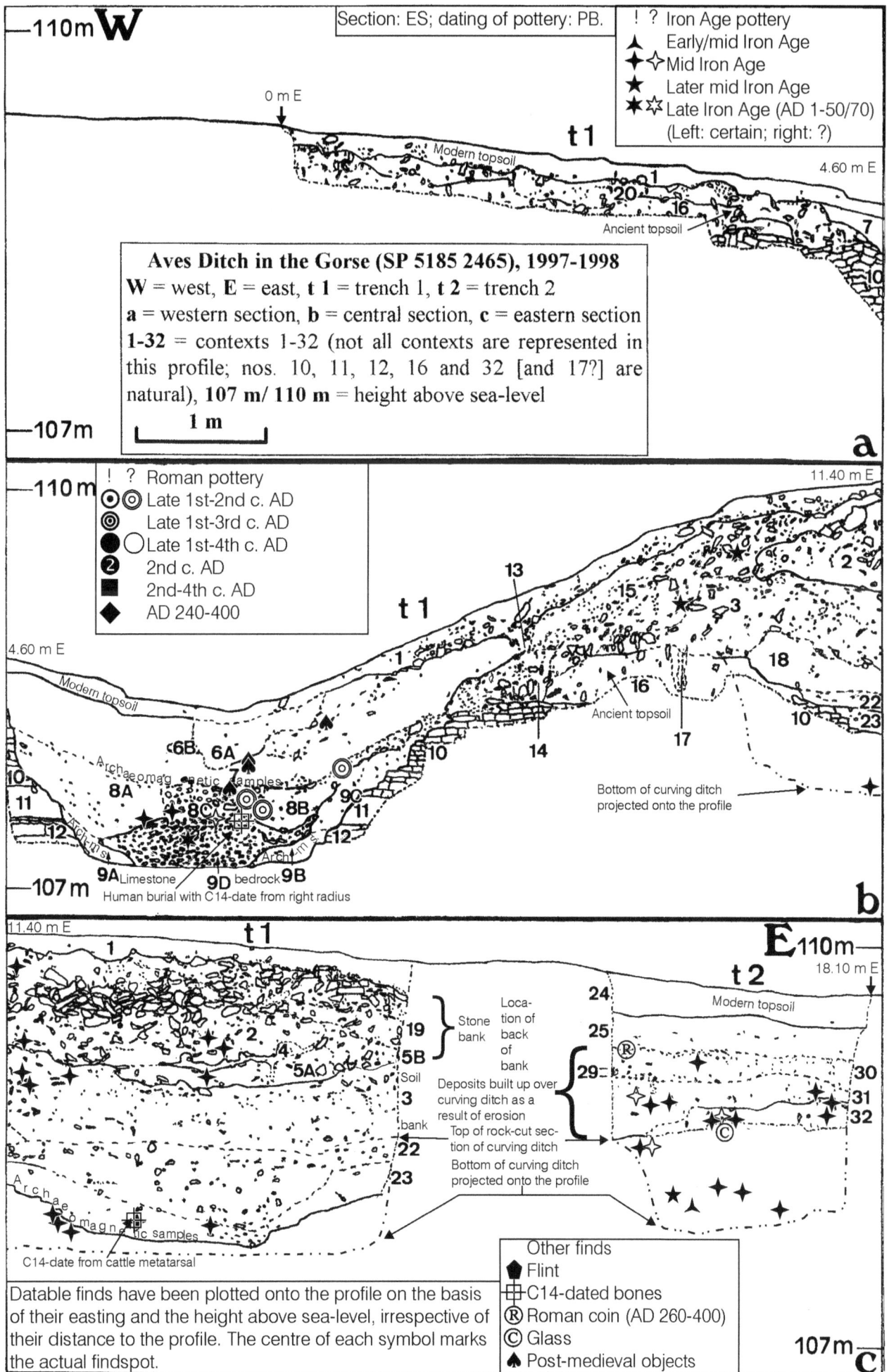

Figure 16. Section of trenches 1 and 2 along the profile line (see **fig. 13**). The numbers refer to contexts. The eastings and heights correspond to the small find 3Ds listed in tables 3 and 4. Post-medieval objects embedded in deposits 1 and 6A have not been plotted.

15

son's examination (below) of the molluscs from context 23, the enclosure appears to have been situated in a cleared landscape, so that there probably would have been no scarcity of pasture for the animals.

The archaeomagnetic date (if reliable), furnishes a *terminus ad quem* of c. 500-325 BC for the earliest ditch fill (context 23). It is worth noting that the samples were taken 3-8 cm above the bottom of the deposit in the south-facing profile, which corresponds to some 14-31 cm above the bottom of the curving ditch; despite being up to a foot above the bottom, material would have been washed into the ditch down the slope, and the position of the samples thus suggests that they represent an early phase of the silting up of the ditch. A radiocarbon date from a cattle metatarsal provides a *terminus post quem* of 770-410 BC (**figs 16 and 17**). These two dates (both discussed in more detail in 'The date of Aves Ditch') suggest that the enclosure ditch had started to silt up at the latest between 500 and 325 BC (or, probably, 500 and 410 BC, as it seems more likely that the cattle bone belonged to an animal kept or slaughtered in the enclosure rather than being an earlier random loss) and was, presumably, constructed shortly before.

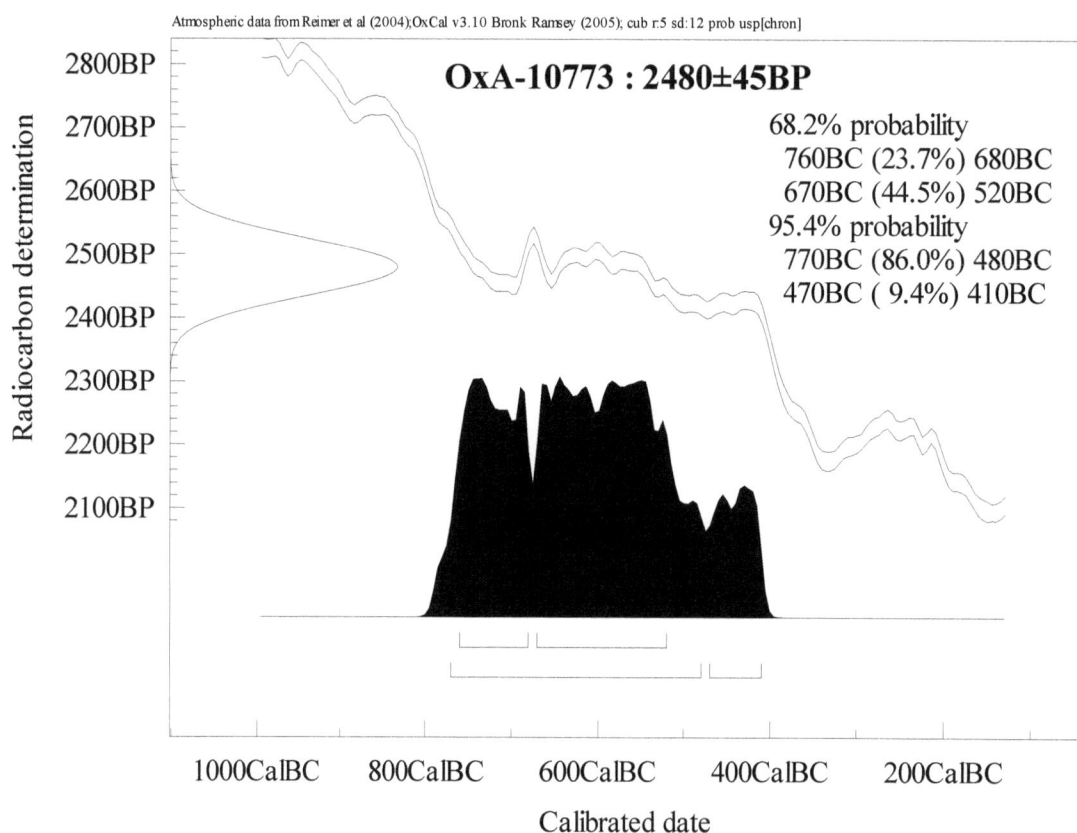

Figure 17. The radiocarbon sample from a cattle metatarsal from context 23 (OxA-10773: 2480±45 BP) kindly provided by Dr Tom Higham (RLAHA, University of Oxford).

The Aves Ditch enclosure is thus earlier than the two excavated Banjo enclosures, at Micheldever and Wherwell; and so is the pottery spectrum, dominated in the curving ditch at Aves Ditch by mid Iron Age sherds, whereas in the other two examples late Iron Age pottery predominates, although mid Iron Age sherds are present (Hawkes 1987: 37 tab. 7; Cunliffe and Poole 2000: 135). It may not be without interest to note that the dominance of sheep/ goat at our site (see Knight below) is matched in mid Iron Age deposits at Micheldever (Coy 1987). Yet, since our enclosure is not a neat representative of this type of enclosure, if a representative at all, and located in a different region, not too much should be read into such comparisons.

Other irregular enclosures are visible on aerial photographs to the south-west of trenches 1 and 2 and to the west of the linear earthwork (**fig. 15**; SP 5124/5-7, NMR 15119/14-16 and SP 5124/9-13, NMR 15112/26 & 28-31 of 12/7/1994), but differential land use on either side of Aves Ditch made it impossible to see whether or not they were confined to this side. Sebastian Rahtz and Trevor Rowley (1984: 4 fig. 3, 155-6) interestingly refer to a cluster of late Iron Age and Roman (first to fourth-century) pottery near the intersection of a brook and Aves Ditch, just south of the point where the modern Middleton Stoney - Lower Heyford road cuts through the earthwork (**fig. 6**). This suggests that settlement existed close to the trenches we excavated in 1997/98. No information on the precise location of this pottery cluster could be obtained beyond the information provided in the report, but, if associated with the enclosures, it would point to the existence of a later settlement in immediate vicinity of the earthwork. Modern tree cover and meadows west of trenches 1 and 2 render the area unsuitable for aerial survey or field walking, and we thus do not know whether the settlement extended further north and, if so, how close it came to our trenches. While the existence of mid Iron Age or Roman enclosures immediately to the west of the earthwork would not interfere with its postulated interpretation as a boundary earthwork (see section on 'A tribal boundary?' below), a contemporary occupation in the late Iron Age immediately outside it might. However, in the absence of sufficiently secure dating and location of the pottery scatter, little would be gained by speculating whether or not the associated settlement was affected by the construction of Aves Ditch, if originating earlier and still occupied, or influenced by its course, if later. There was just a single late Iron Age sherd from our 1997/98 trenches (**fig. 16**), but the stronger representation of Roman pottery may be significant. Whether this pottery derives from the same (larger?) settlement or a second cluster closer to our trenches, is unknown.

As this report is going into print, excavations by Cotswold Archaeology along a pipeline trench in immediate vicinity of Aves Ditch are being completed. These promise to shed significant new light on the date and function of the enclosures and other traces of settlement near the Gorse. These excavations may answer some of the questions raised in this chapter, but their results could not be taken into consideration here and one awaits with anticipation the forthcoming report.

THE CONSTRUCTION OF AVES DITCH

No find from the bottom fill of the curving ditch (**fig. 16**) post-dates the later mid Iron Age (even if much or all of this may derive from the enclosure). The high stone contents of the upper fill of the curving ditch (deposits 22, 35 and 36), as opposed to the very low percentage of stones in the bottom fill (contexts 23 and 37), suggest that it survived as a distinct depression until it was deliberately filled up. This happened most probably just before the construction of Aves Ditch to remove this obstacle in the way of the marked-out route. The high proportion of stones may have been deliberate to prevent later subsidence. The bottom of the bank built on top of it consists of a soft mid-reddish brown clayey silt with a low (c. 5-15%) stone content (contexts 3 and 18), almost certainly re-deposited ancient topsoil from the higher levels of what was to become the ditch. The upper part of the bank (contexts 2 and 19) showed a much higher stone concentration (**figs 16, 18 and 19**). The transition between stone and soil bank is not very sharp, suggesting that during the construction of the earthwork some labourers had already reached the bedrock and brought quarried stones onto the bank, whereas others still extracted material from the upper section of the ditch or from the ancient topsoil in the surroundings. The core of context 2 consisted of large loosely packed limestone blocks,

Figure 18. Section through Aves Ditch on 7 December 1997. Note that the bottom of the ditch or the natural had not been reached, but the WNW-facing rock-cut side of the ditch is clearly visible. Each segment of the scales (excl. the pointed tips) measures 500 mm.

Figure 19. A one-metre section of the bank prior to excavation of the curving ditch on 13 December 1997. The stone bank consisting of large limestone blocks is clearly visible. The two vertical scales are at 12.12 and 13.12 m E. Each segment of the scales (excl. the pointed tips) measures 500 mm.

which must have been quarried from the lower ditch. Sizeable air pockets between the stones, such as tend to occur when large blocks are piled up within a short period of time, remained in the lower part of the stone bank (context 2), but not in the upper sections (context 19). The pressure caused by walkers, animals and later wheeled traffic, as well as root action and animal activity, will have caused the cavities close to the surface to be filled with soil and stones, but even some two millennia did not eliminate air pockets at a lower level. The sloping layering of stones in context 15 suggests strongly that this deposit was created as a result of the erosion of the bank. The preserved west face of the bank is thus likely to coincide with that of context 3. Prior to its erosion, it would, almost certainly, have been steeper.

No traces of a timber framework were observed in 1997/98. Context 17 in trench 1 [**fig. 16**] is probably natural rather than a posthole. In 1937, however, one possible posthole came to light in trench II, half a metre away from the upper eastern lip of the ditch, i.e. on the side of the bank (**fig. 23**). (Theoretically, it would be in an ideal position for the front of a timber framework, if we could be certain that it was a posthole and that it belonged to the same phase as the earthwork.) In the light of the narrowness of our trench 1, it cannot be excluded that there were postholes at wider intervals for such a framework, but in the absence of firm comparative evidence from any other contemporary linear earthwork in the area, it seems unlikely (cf., however, Hinchliffe's [1976: 133] theory that the South Oxfordshire Grim's Ditch may have had a timber revetment destroyed by later chalk quarrying). We equally found no traces of a palisade trench along Aves Ditch. It is worth noting, however, that some of the potential palisade trenches in front of the North Oxfordshire Grim's Ditch, on the side opposite to the bank (Harding 1972: 57-8; Thomas 1958: 16, 25-6, figs 6-7; Harden 1937: 80-1, figs A-B), were at a sufficiently great distance outside the ditch that we could have missed any potential palisade trench in a similar position in our trench 1, which extended only some 4.50 m beyond the western edge of the ditch (**fig. 16**). The same is true for the 1937 trenches, which covered even less ground west of the ditch (**fig. 23**).

We do not know what tools were used to excavate Aves Ditch. Its flat bottom in trench 1 (**figs 16, 20 and 21**) was found to be so hard that it required c. 10 to 15 strong blows with a modern pick-axe to take a stone sample. The sides seemed slightly softer and it seems possible that the flat bottom of the ditch coincides with the surface of a particularly hard layer of bedrock. Nevertheless, when we deliberately over-cut the edges of the ditch, in order to be absolutely sure that we have reached the real edges on both sides, we removed some solid bedrock. Particularly towards the bottom of the trench this proved to be extremely hard work, even with modern pickaxes and mattocks. Should Aves Ditch be an early Roman military earthwork or a road, then iron entrenchment tools (*dolabrae*) of similar quality to our modern tools would probably have been in plentiful supply. If it dates back to the late Iron Age, then the question of what equipment was used is more difficult to answer. Suitable Iron tools, such as picks and adzes, had already been available well before the conquest (Sellwood 1984a, 351, 353-4; Croom 2001: 141-2), but in the light of their comparative scarcity we should not necessarily assume that Aves Ditch was excavated by a team equipped with iron tools. We observed no tool marks to provide clues to the type of equipment used for cutting the ditch in the bedrock. It seems fair to conclude that the decision to cut a ditch through the hard limestone bedrock in the Middleton Stoney/ Upper Heyford area would not have been taken casually and without strong motives, even if we are dealing with forced labour, rather than a project carried out by a local community for some recognised shared benefit. In either case, the workforce required could have been, undoubtedly, usefully employed to carry out even more substantial construction works elsewhere, in areas with a less demanding geology.

While our ignorance of the equipment used hampers any attempt to gain an idea of the time and efforts required to build this monument, the Overton Experimental Earthwork project still provides an interesting parallel. We cannot, of course, be certain that the speed achieved by a

Figure 20. The extended trench 1 on 22 June 1998 seen from the north-west: the rock-cut ditch is on the right, the bank on the left. Each segment of the scale (excl. the pointed tip) measures 500 mm.

Figure 21. The NNE-facing profile of the rock-cut flat-bottomed ditch on 22 June 1998. Each segment of the scales (excl. the pointed tips) measures 500 mm. The vertical scale is split into sections of 10 x 10 mm; each 'E'-shaped symbol or its mirror image corresponds to 5 x 10 mm.

modern team (whose members varied in fitness and experience), when excavating a ditch in chalk and building a bank of the spoil (with antler picks, ox and horse scapulae and wicker baskets) matched that achieved in limestone (especially since we cannot be sure what tools were used by the labourers creating Aves Ditch); if anything, the limestone would have posed a significantly greater challenge. (For most of its course, the 4.2 km-long straight section of Aves Ditch is cut into Great Oolite Limestone, while in the southern third the bedrock consists of Forest Marble and Cornbrash [Geological Survey of Great Britain, England and Wales, Sheet 218 (Southampton 1968)].) Nevertheless, the average speed on Overton Down for people of all age groups and levels of experience was three cubic feet per hour and about five cubic feet for fit and experienced team members (Jewell 1963: 50-8, pl. VIII). We can estimate, on the basis of the original surface and the profile and depth of the ditch in the area of trench 1, that 5.8 m^3 of stones and soil had to be dug out and shifted per one metre length of Aves Ditch. If we assume that the earthwork ran for the entire 4.2 km without gaps and had originally similar dimensions all way through (neither of which is certain), this would equate to 24,360 m^3 or 860,265 cubic feet for the 4.2 km. On the assumption of similar working speed in the earthmoving operations at Aves Ditch as at Overton, the 4.2 km would have taken some 170,000 to 290,000 hours to construct, or 100 people working 215 to 360 8-hour days. (The geology of Aves Ditch and steep gradient of the evolving slope between ditch bottom and top of the bank probably excludes, at least for lower sections of the ditch and the stone bank, the technique of scraping soil backwards as described by Burl [1991: 19] on the basis of a Nigerian parallel.) Needless to say that a team equipped with iron tools, especially if consisting of trained Roman soldiers, would have been somewhat faster. It is worth noting that the figures above do not take the possible continuation of the linear monument between Chilgrove Drive (the lane from north of 'The Heath' to the now-destroyed Ballard's Copse on **fig. 8**) and Fritwell into account.

THE DATE OF AVES DITCH

A radiocarbon date from a, probably re-deposited, cattle metatarsal recovered from the curving ditch filled in prior to the construction of the linear earthwork (770-410 BC or 760-520 BC at 95.4% or 68.2% probability respectively [OxA-10773: 2480±45 BP]) (**fig. 17**) provides a firm *terminus post quem* for the construction of the earthwork. A second carbon-14 date, from the right radius of a skeleton buried within the main ditch, (AD 670-870 or AD 685-780 at 95.4% or 68.2% probability respectively [OxA-13729: 1254±30 BP]) (**fig. 36**) provides a firm *terminus ante quem* (**fig. 16**). The same is true for the archaeomagnetic dates (see Patrick Erwin below, **fig. 41**) from the bottom silt (context 23) of the curving ditch (500-325 BC) and from the bottom of context 7 (AD 275-550). These scientific dates are of great relevance for the curving ditch and the associated enclosure as well as for the later burial; however, they are of lesser significance for the history of the linear earthwork itself, allowing for a date range of over a millennium for its construction.

Crucial for the dating of Aves Ditch is the pottery (see Booth below). Context and three-dimensional position of sherds and other datable small finds were recorded in our excavations. Fortunately, already in 1937 the findspots of all sherds had been recorded and plotted onto the section drawings; the numbered finds have been kept in the Ashmolean Museum to the present day, so that it was possible to correlate individual objects with their stratigraphic position. Notwithstanding the, at least partial, misattribution of the pottery to the Roman period in the original publication (Anon. 1937), the diligence of the recording system has enabled us to correct this mistake. We thus have reasonably sizeable pottery assemblages from both, the three 1937 trenches and the 1997/98 section, some four kilometres apart. (It is worth noting that, while we have a location plan for trench II and III [**fig. 22**] at and near the southern ditch and bank terminals, we have no plan or description for the location of trench I, another section through the earthwork further north; it seems likely that it was near the other two trenches excavated in 1937, but we do not know where precisely. All the fieldwork appears to have taken place 'at the S. end of the Ditch as marked on O.S. 6-inch Oxon. XXII' map (**fig. 7**) within Kirtlington parish (Anon. 1937; cf. 1938: 185).

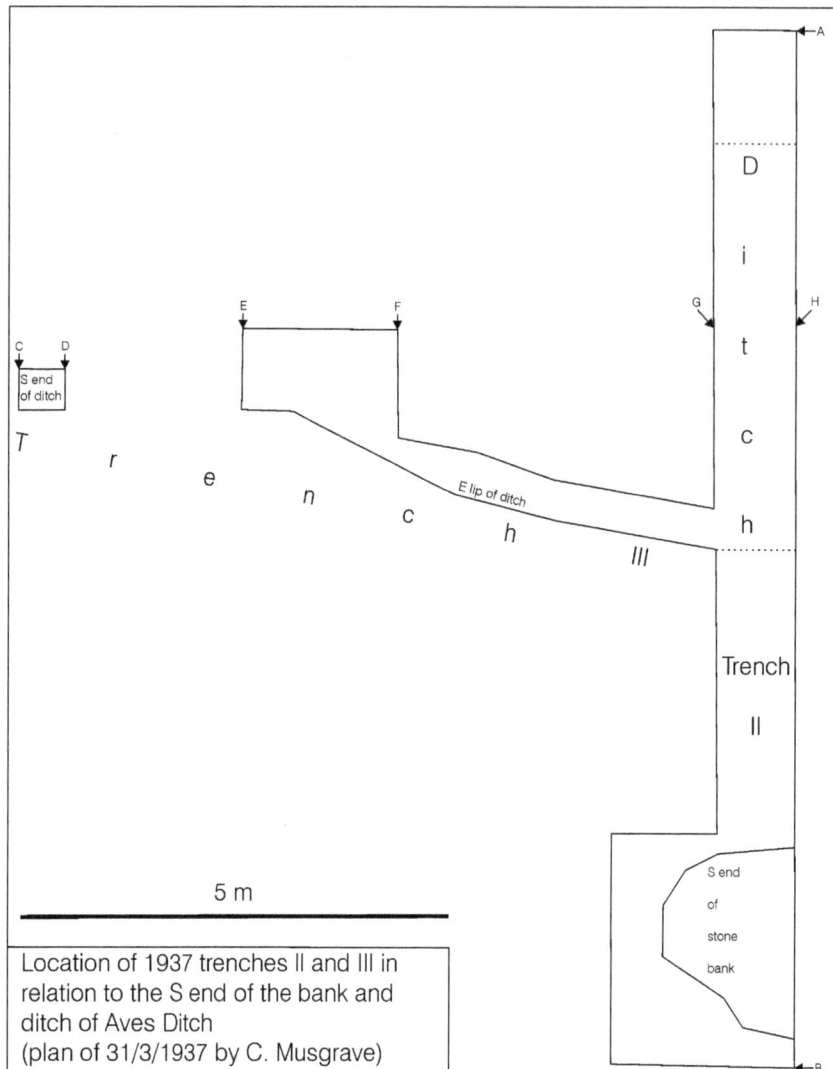

Figure 22. Plan of trenches II and III at the southern terminals of the bank and ditch of the earthwork.
Note that the precise location of trench I has not been recorded.

It is important to note that not a single certain Roman or post-Roman sherd or other object was found embedded into the bank of even bottom silt of the ditch of the linear earthwork in any of these trenches. The higher proportion of mid, as opposed to late, Iron Age sherds from the 1997/98 (**fig. 16**), in comparison with the 1937 (**fig. 23**), excavations is likely to be the result of the re-deposition of material from the earlier enclosure in the vicinity of trenches 1 and 2 (as pointed out above). Some late Iron Age finds could in theory, of course, still have been discarded within a generation after the conquest of AD 43, while no diagnostic Roman objects need have been lost within the first few months or years of Roman rule; the absence of distinctive Roman sherds, not only from the bank, but even from the later bottom silt of the ditch argues, in any case, against a construction date several decades or more after the Roman invasion.

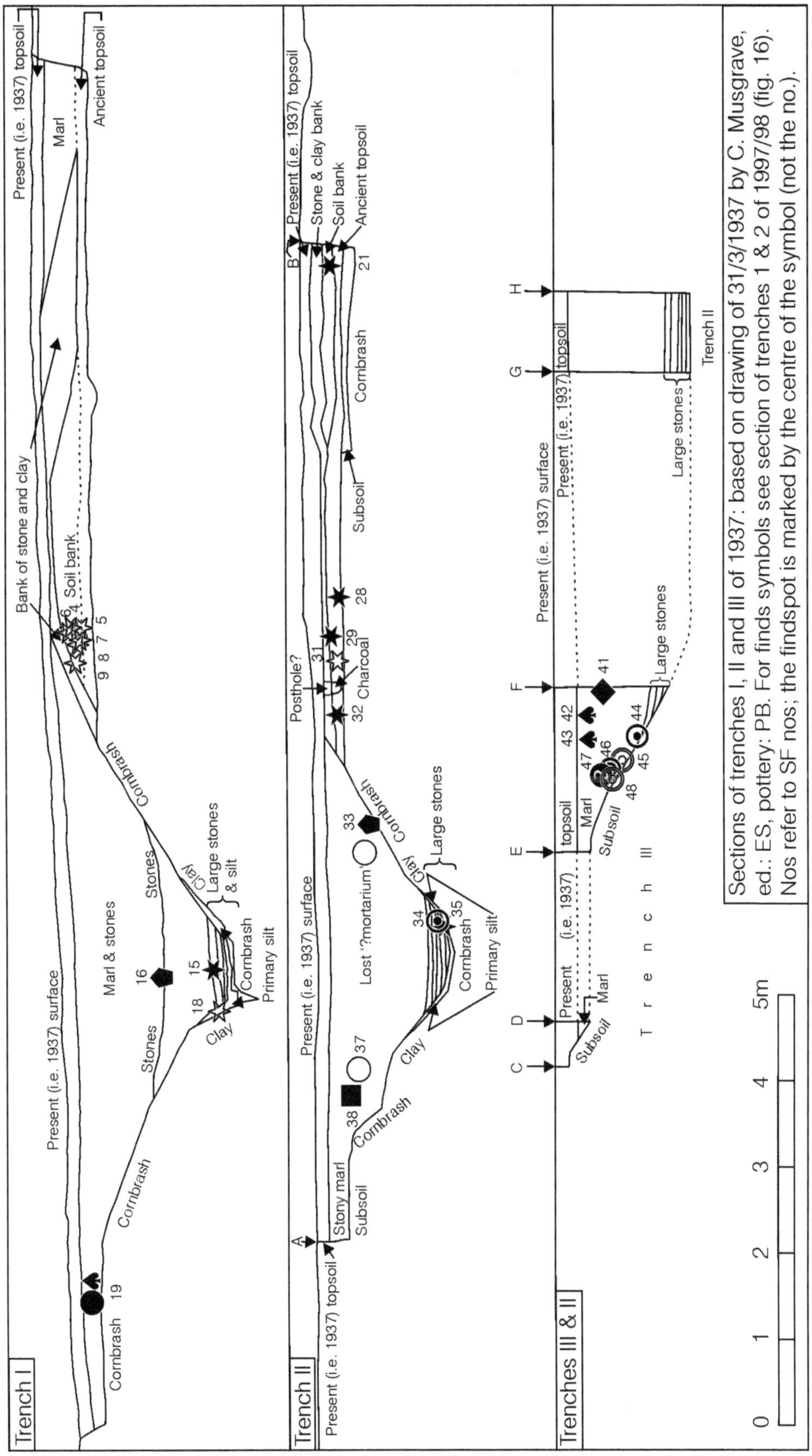

Figure 23. Sections of trenches I, II and III excavated in 1937. The numbers refer to pottery sherds listed in Paul Booth's report (tables 7, 8 and 9).

Even if an early military pottery spectrum is a highly unreliable indicator for the composition of contemporary civilian spectra in the hinterland, it may be worth noting that the fabrics encountered at Aves Ditch are distinctively different from the copious material found at the Alchester fortress established as early as AD 43/44 (Sauer 2005 with references) and at a mere 7 km from Aves Ditch. The quantity of datable sherds and the physical distance between the trenches renders it extremely unlikely that the absence of Roman sherds from construction or pre-construction deposits in all six trenches could be coincidental. While a construction date in the immediate post-conquest period cannot be ruled out with certainty, it is hard to imagine that it was built in the later first, let alone subsequent centuries. Even if it is impossible to generalise, as the absence or presence and density of finds of any particular period in any one section of a bank of an earthwork is crucially dependent on the activity in the periods predating its construction in the immediate surroundings, it is worth noting that some later earthworks in southern Britain have yielded substantial quantities of re-deposited Roman artefacts from sections through their bank (see, for example, Castle 1975).

The frequency of late Iron Age pottery from the bank in two of the 1937 trenches on the other hand argues against a construction of the earth-work at the very beginning of the first century AD, let alone prior to the turn of the century; it seems more likely that we are dealing with a date in, or not long before, the second quarter of the first century.

The archaeomagnetic dates from the bottom of the associated linear ditch (contexts (9A and B) were, unfortunately, off curve, but it is interesting, nevertheless, that Patrick Erwin's independent tentative dating proposal of 250 BC to AD 150 (see Erwin below and Erwin 1999a and b) coincides with Paul Booth's more precise (and subsequent) pottery chronology (see Booth below).

A ROAD OR A BOUNDARY MARKER?

In order to examine further whether the construction date of the linear earthwork is more likely to fall shortly before or shortly after the Roman conquest, we need to consider its likely function and possible parallels. Its straightness and orientation towards the ford at Tackley, at which Akeman Street crosses the river Cherwell, have given rise to the theory that it was a road (see references above). According to the 1937 excavations (Anon. 1937; cf. **figs 22, 23 and 9**), however, the bank and ditch came to terminals some 1.2 km before reaching the ford. Before these terminals had been found, O'Neil (1929: 33) believed he could discern the bank of Aves Ditch, maintaining the same alignment, beyond this point, since 'here and there a rise is noticeable proceeding in the right direction.' When nearing Crowcastle Lane (a public footpath from Kirtlington to Northbrook [plotted, though not named, on **figs 4 and 9**]) 'this rise bears farther to the south and appears not to cross the Lane but to join it.' O'Neil observed no trace of a road between the Lane and the river and points to the presence of a 'deep bifurcated coombe', which would indeed have made a direct continuation difficult. If the (discontinuous?) rise O'Neil observed was indeed a continuation of Aves Ditch, then travellers heading in a southwards direction beyond the postulated junction would have reached the ford following a section of Crowcastle Lane and of Akeman Street, i.e. via a less direct route than a theoretical prolongation of Aves Ditch to the ford would have offered. The distinct terminals of ditch and bank unearthed in 1937, however, are not easy to reconcile with a road running on for another 500 m (and neither am I aware of any aerial photographs showing clear traces of this postulated additional stretch, though see **fig. 1** for an ill-defined [unrelated or ploughed-out?] positive crop mark in a similar alignment beyond the terminal). On an, admittedly brief, inspection on the ground in June 2005 of what was visible from a driveway O'Neil's postulated rise should have crossed, I observed no traces of any bank or road, despite the grass being short and a reasonable stretch of land being visible from this drive-way. We should, nevertheless, not exclude the possibility of a discontinuous road-side quarry ditch and a partially destroyed *agger* (i.e. the causeway formed by a Roman road), short of further excavations, geophysical or topographical surveys deciding the question one way or the other. At present, however, the balance of the evidence is rather against the existence of such a link between the monument and Tackley ford. If greater reliance is placed on the 1937 excavations than on the, so far, unconfirmed observations of 1929, then the constructors of Aves Ditch, had they intended it to be a road, either never finished construction works, or the stretch between the end of the stone bank and its postulated junction with Akeman Street at Tackley ford down the slope of the valley must have been a short-lived unpaved track, which never evolved into a hollow way or left any other trace in the landscape, recognised as such to date. The absence, as far as I am aware, of any firm evidence on the ground for its existence indicates that such a track, if there ever was one, cannot have been used extensively for a longer period of time. Unless O'Neil's 'rise' should indeed be proven to be the continuation of Aves Ditch's bank in future, then the stone bank, thought by many to be the *agger* of a road, seems to start in the 'middle of nowhere' in the south.

Figure 24. Trench 3 under excavation on 2 August 1998 seen from the south-west: scarcely visible in the high grass is the parish boundary bank on the left; the eastern half of it is sectioned and it is marked by a line of stones immediately under the topsoil.

In this context it is essential to explore how far Aves Ditch extended in the north. It is frequently thought to run along Chilgrove Drive (the road from the 'Heath' northwards) and Raghouse Lane to Fritwell or beyond (**figs 4 and 8**; Atkinson and McKenzie 1946-1947; Beesley 1841: 29, 38-9, pl. IV; Blomfield 1882: map facing p. 21; Lobel 1959: 135; Potts 1907: 342); some of these sections are within the, now-abandoned, Upper Heyford airfield or had been destroyed already before (Blomfield 1882: 25). However, our trench 3 (**figs 6 and 24**) suggests that the stone bank of the straight section comes to a similar sudden end in the north as in the south and that the ditch does not continue to the north. We found no remains of the ditch or bank (gun cartridges being the most ancient artefacts recovered from this trench).

A partial section, at the western end of this trench, of a small bank marking the parish boundary, yielded no ancient artefacts, and its construction, profile and (much more modest) dimensions (rising to a height of merely 400-500 mm above the surrounding terrain) bear no similarities to the Iron Age bank further south. This was the only manmade feature encountered in this 7.80 m long trench, even though the natural was reached along its entire length; in sections we even dug up to 500 mm deep into the natural to verify that we were not dealing with re-deposited stones. It ought to be stressed that the location of this trench had been based on the assumption that, if anything, this bank was the only conceivable feature in the area marking the continuation of the earthwork to the north. This seemed justified as no traces of a straight continuation of the ditch or bank of Aves Ditch are visible on the ground in the area, nor to the east of trench 3, where one would expect them. With the benefit of hindsight, it would have been desirable to extend the trench a few more metres to the east. If, contrary to our assumption, Aves Ditch continued in a straight alignment, but was completely levelled, then we might have narrowly missed the western edge of the ditch. In the absence of any surviving or mapped landscape feature in straight continuation of Aves Ditch east of trench 3 or further north, it seems likely that the terminal of its straight section was indeed to the south of the trench. This hypothesis could easily be tested with a small trench in future.

Earlier attempts to find archaeological proof of a continuation of the earthwork at Fritwell have equally been unsuccessful (Chambers 1993: 44-6, 49, 51; Morse 1995). The absence of positive evidence for the monument reaching or crossing modern Fritwell, does not disprove the possibility that some of the intervening sections could have been a continuation of the earthwork northwards, albeit no longer following alignments as straight as the southernmost 4.2 km under discussion here. Notably sections of Chilgrove Drive (the lane from north of 'The Heath' to the now-destroyed Ballard's Copse on **fig. 8**) and Raghouse Lane, as well as in Kennel Copse in between, in places still form a slightly elevated causeway today. As it has carried traffic for a long time and is now paved throughout, it is impossible to establish how much higher the bank might have been originally. Interestingly, parts of Chilgrove Drive and Raghouse Lane form, like a section of Aves Ditch further south, parish boundaries. This, however, provides no certain clue as to the original function of the monument; different linear landscape features, Roman roads as well as boundary dykes, formed suitable landmarks for local subdivisions of territory. As none of the sections cut through this earthwork or this ancient road in the course of construction works has, to my knowledge, ever been recorded, we cannot compare its construction with that of the southern straight earthwork, nor is there independent dating evidence for Chilgrove Drive or Raghouse Lane. It seems possible, nevertheless, that they may indeed be part of Aves Ditch, even though there is a gap between the Gorse and Chilgrove Drive. It is equally possible that after the postulated transformation of Aves Ditch from an earthwork into a local road, this could have been further extended in the north. The track and road crossing modern Fritwell from south to north might be such a secondary feature.

While it would be most unusual for a road to consist of discontinuous stretches of massive causeways with major gaps in between, for no obvious topographical reasons, if Aves Ditch formed an artificial boundary, then any wood or scrubland at the slopes of the Cherwell Valley may have made it unnecessary to prolong the earthwork into the valley. Similarly, possible areas of impenetrable vegetation in antiquity may have determined its end in the north, or its continuation could have been formed by a hedge. That such natural obstacles may have filled gaps in earthworks has also been suggested for the nearby North Oxfordshire Grim's Ditch (Harden 1937: 90, cf. 75; Harding 1972: 58; Copeland 1989: 283) and literary evidence provides analogies to strengthen such a hypothesis (cf. below under 'Artificial barriers at tribal and political boundaries'). By contrast, it would have made no sense for a road to have an arbitrary 4.2 km section paved without any continuation on either side and without any obvious topographical reason for the location of either terminal of the paved section. If Aves

Ditch ever was intended to be a road, then it was never completed. Indeed, it terminates without any recognisable direct continuation and without reaching, or leading to the vicinity of, any significant known settlement of the time; there is no obvious destination. This weakness in its interpretation as a road is also acknowledged by Margary (1973: 168).

There appears to be no evidence on the ground for the claim that the southern section of Aves Ditch (i.e. the 4.2 km long straight section under discussion here) 'is part of a Roman road evidently to connect Cirencester with Towcester via Akeman Street' (Hargreaves *et al.* 1974: 10, cf. 11). Neither is there an obvious explanation why a second road, so close to the Alchester - Towcester road, should have been considered necessary for the travellers between Tackley ford and Towcester. Assuming that there was nevertheless a perceived need in antiquity, on the basis that the only known part of this postulated road appears to be this stretch of Aves Ditch, and without a substantial reason why the remainder of such a causewayed road should have vanished without a trace, it seems doubtful that such an alternative traffic link between Towcester and Tackley ford ever existed.

A further argument against the interpretation of Aves Ditch as a road, even as one abandoned when it was less than half-finished, is its, for this purpose, unnecessarily labour-intensive construction. The preserved height differential between the bottom of the ditch and the top of the bank, in the area of trench 1, amounts to almost three metres (**fig. 16**). This is well in excess of the main west-east road in the area, Akeman Street (Harden 1939: 273 fig. 18) and, indeed, most roads in Roman Britain (Margary 1973: 500-1). As the bottom 0.60 m of the ditch fill consists of re-deposited material from the stone bank, there is little doubt that this figure must originally have been over three metres. The height differential between the preserved top of the bank and the bottom of the ditch in the 1937 trenches is slightly less. Since only the bank remains are less elevated, while the ditch is of similar dimensions in trench I as it is in trench 1 and only slightly less deep and wide in trench II, close to its southern terminal, this may be the result of plough damage, already reported to severely affect the southernmost sections by the beginning of the last century (Potts 1907: 342); originally, the bank in the southern sections of Aves Ditch was probably of proportions comparable to those observed near its northern terminal. On the well-drained plateau, there would have been no need for such a massive construction for what could have been only a very minor road, if a road at all.

It might be objected, however, that the massive remains of Aves Ditch in the area of trenches 1 and 2 in the Gorse are not far from the intersection of the earthwork and a (nowadays, at least, minor) stream. The question thus arises whether the presence of the massive causeway in the vicinity of a stream crossing (to allow passage in all seasons?) does not offer support for an explanation of Aves Ditch as a road. However, a comparison between the preserved height of the *agger* of Aves Ditch of c. 1.28 m above the top of the ancient topsoil (context 16) in trench 1 (**fig. 16**) in the Gorse, some 125 m NNE of its intersection with a minor stream (**fig. 6**) and the preserved height of Akeman Street of 0.46 m, '1 ft. 6 in. at most above normal river level' (O'Neil 1929: 30), just 5 m east of the much more substantial river Cherwell, speaks for itself, especially in the light of O'Neil's (1929) view that preserved brushwood in the foundation of Akeman Street indicates a similar water table of the Cherwell in the Roman period. By contrast, the top of the bank of Aves Ditch in trench 1 is still today over 110 m above the sea-level and, while no precise figures for the water level in the stream were available at the time of writing, it is in any case well below 106 m. It is thus obvious that the bank of Aves Ditch in trench 1 is several metres above maximum conceivable flood levels, and that merely to allow dry passage in all seasons cannot have been the motive for constructing such an elevated bank. There is no evidence from any other section of Aves Ditch either that the purpose of its massive construction was to facilitate the crossing of streams. While the bank of Aves Ditch is well-preserved north-north-east of its intersection with a minor (and in June 2005 dry) stream in Goldwell Spinney (**fig. 7**), it is no more massive than it is at many other sections between this point and our trenches 1 and 2. Furthermore, Aves Ditch reaches substantial dimensions in the area of the 1937 trenches, where there is no risk of flooding at all. As it is possible that Chilgrove Drive and Raghouse Lane may form a part of Aves Ditch, it is worth noting that they display the same pattern: whilst still slightly raised, the causeway is no more pronounced at the two intersections with minor streams than on average elsewhere (even if not too much reliance should be placed that what survives at present of this, quite heavily used, causeway reflects its original shape).

Figure 25. Ackling Dyke in Dorset is exceptional for a Roman road in having been provided with such a massive *agger*.

Aves Ditch seems to be too substantial a construction for a Roman road, let alone a minor side route. This even holds true if one postulates that the deep ditch had been dug as a road-side quarry ditch for the much wider and less elevated *agger* and is unconcerned about the absence of a ditch on the eastern side, even if it would be unusual for a road of this period to have only one ditch. Few Roman roads, other than Ackling Dyke in Dorset (**fig. 25**), come to mind which match the ditch-*agger* height differential of Aves Ditch. Ackling Dyke (with its even much more massive *agger*, but, unlike Aves Ditch, two drainage ditches) in equally dry terrain may have served as a symbolic statement in the landscape for Rome's power (Margary 1973: 104-5 no. 4c, pls III-IVA). Yet, if Aves Ditch was intended to serve a similar function, though never to be completed and without parallel in the area, its location would be odd: the 4.2 km-long straight section of Aves Ditch is not crossed by any other significant ancient traffic route, except for the Port Way (**figs 4 and 7**), and is not in the immediate vicinity of any major settlement; it seems unlikely in the extreme that such a hypothetical labour-intensive demonstration of power would have been erected in a stretch of land where only a handful of peasants were ever likely to see it.

Despite its orientation toward the ford used by Akeman Street, the main west-east road, it seems thus more likely that Aves Ditch was originally intended to be an earthwork rather than a road. There is clear evidence that the ford was in use at the beginning of Roman rule and probably before: the west-east road at Alchester, leading through a gate of AD 44 (Sauer 2001: 2 fig. 1, 14; 2002: 355; Booth *et al.* 2002: 3 fig. 1.2), equally points towards Tackley ford. This observation furthermore suggests that in AD 44 Akeman Street, half a kilometre north of Alchester, was not intended to be the main west-east road and that it originated either earlier or later. The fact that its course appears to be respected by the late Iron Age North Oxfordshire Grim's Ditch (Harden 1937: 91; Sauer 1998: 74; Copeland 2002: 75), points to an Iron Age origin of this traffic axis. This would not be surprising, as some of the earliest Roman roads in Gaul are also thought to follow broadly major pre-Roman traffic routes (Metzler 1995: 604). If so, the orientation of Aves Ditch towards the ford and landmark need not imply a post-conquest date, even if it provides evidence for advanced surveying skills of those in charge of its construction, as does its remarkable straightness.

It is, incidentally, interesting to note that the westernmost section of the A4095 (the road with a spot height of 323 feet on **fig. 4**) which branches off the eastern side of the old Port Way (**fig. 4**), some 900 m south of its intersection with Aves Ditch, would also reach the Cherwell c. 100 m north of Tackley ford, if prolonged to the west (but, unlike Akeman Street and the alignments of Aves Ditch and, probably, the AD-40s west-east road, it would clearly miss the ford). There is no obvious topographical reason why the alignments of sections of the A4095 bend successively further and further to the south, unless it was intended to reach the ford (which it apparently never did). No speculation will be offered here as to what, if anything, this tells us about the antiquity and original function of the predecessor of the A4095, but it is interesting to note that three (or, possibly, with the A4095, four) linear ancient landscape features east of the Cherwell seem to be orientated towards this one particular ford. Why their alignments seem to radiate from the ford in an easterly to north-easterly direction, but why, apart from Akeman Street (Benson and Harding 1968; O'Neil 1929; Margary 1973: 159), none can be shown to have come anywhere close to the ford (unless evidence should emerge for O'Neil's above-quoted tentatively identified link between the Aves Ditch's terminal and the ford), remains a mystery.

If Aves Ditch was a linear earthwork, it seems unlikely that it was a private boundary (e.g. of an estate or an enclosure for wild or domesticated animals), as this would probably not just have been on one side of privately owned land. More probably, it would have marked or protected a communal boundary or frontier zone. If so, two principal options present themselves: it was either (1.) a late Iron Age installation or (2.) it was an early Roman creation, perhaps, associated with the Alchester fortress, with the aim of controlling traffic from the west.

A ROMAN LINEAR BARRIER?

The vicinity of the Alchester fortress (2.5 km south-west of Bicester, cf. **fig. 28**) raises the attractive option that Aves Ditch may indeed have been an early warning system to slow down any hostile advances and to alarm the garrison of this invasion-period complex; the west and north, of course, were the most likely directions, from which to expect an attack. Linear barriers, notably Hadrian's Wall, are amongst the most labour-intensive monuments constructed in the Roman world, and the earthworks associated with some them, such as the Antonine Wall in Britain and the German 'Limes' in Germania Superior, are similar in construction to Aves Ditch. Yet, while these linear monuments represent the epitome of Roman military architecture to the modern public, it ought to be borne in mind that none of the above-mentioned Roman walls or other earthwork barriers in their developed form, i.e. with a ditch plus a bank or wall, pre-dates the second century AD. If Aves Ditch was a smaller precursor of mid-first century date, then, for it to function as an early warning system, it would have been necessary to transmit signals from Aves Ditch to Alchester via patrols or undetected timber watchtowers. This, undoubtedly, would have been technically perfectly feasible, but it is nevertheless worth bearing in mind that there is no evidence that anything comparable to the sophisticated signalling and early warning systems along Rome's artificial barriers of the second and third centuries AD already existed in the first century. There appear to have been much more *ad hoc* arrangements in earlier Roman military signalling (Woolliscroft 2001). (Timber watchtowers would be virtually undetectable, short of excavation, unless they were surrounded by a drainage or enclosure ditch. No traces of any such round ditches are visible on aerial photographs of Aves Ditch.).

While, as has been stressed above, virtually none of the other surviving Roman linear military barriers is as early as, or earlier than, Aves Ditch (Napoli 1997: esp. 47; cf. Whittaker 1994: 27, 47-8; Planck 1982), literary evidence attests that linear defences were sporadically created in the late Republican to early imperial period (cf. Napoli 1997: 495-506); there is, however, nothing to suggest that the third-century historian Herodian's testimony (2,11,5) that, under Augustus, the Empire was fortified with ditches, where it lacked natural defences, is anything more than an anachronism. The few pre-Flavian linear barriers more reliably attested in literature appear to have been erected for specific tactical purposes in war, such as Caesar's effective 19 mile-wall and ditch against the Helvetii (Caes., *B. Gall.* 1,8), rather than as part of a medium or long-term defensive system. It is also worth bearing in mind that Roman military ditches tend to have a V-shaped profile, even if the hardness of the limestone bedrock at Middleton Stoney would have made it exceptionally difficult to create a V-shaped ditch. While it is thus not beyond possibility that Aves Ditch could be one of the earliest Roman military linear barriers, maybe erected for a specific tactical purpose as well, the virtual absence of contemporary or earlier parallels renders this rather unlikely.

A TRIBAL BOUNDARY?

If, on the other hand, Aves Ditch was an Iron Age linear earthwork, then the question arises what function it could have served. It is not crossed by any major traffic route, other than the Port Way close to its southern terminal (**figs 4 and 7**), and thus it makes little sense to assume that it was built to control ordinary traffic, and perhaps to levy tolls, as has been plausibly suggested for the (at least partially) early Iron Age dykes blocking the Icknield Way in the eastern Chilterns (Dyer 1961; Bryant 1994: 54, 56). Also the South Oxfordshire Grim's Ditch (Crawford 1931: map facing 168) and many prehistoric or early medieval linear ditches and earthworks located between it and Silchester specifically block traffic routes (O'Neil 1944: map facing 144; cf. 117-22). The South Oxforshire Grim's Ditch itself, however, is distinctively more rectilinear than the other earthworks in the area (**fig. 28**).

It is important to note that the South Oxfordshire Grim's Ditch (**fig. 26**; Hinchliffe 1976: 133-5) and the North Oxfordshire Grim's Ditch (Harden 1937: 82, 89, 91; Copeland 1989: 287; 2002: 52, 61-3) date to roughly the same period as Aves Ditch (i.e. the first half of the first century AD). These three linear earthworks are also remarkably similar in ditch and (where preserved) bank profiles and construction. While there are substantial variations from section to section, even the dimensions of the ditch and (where not destroyed) the bank are often of a comparable order of magnitude (e.g. Harden 1937: pl. 10; Fine 1977: 15 fig. 3; Thomas 1958: fig. 7; Hinchliffe 1976: 127 fig. 4). Aves Ditch and the South Oxfordshire Grim's Ditch, furthermore, share a straight linear alignment, even though the latter does not match the almost geometrical precision of the former (a difference which may result from those marking out the route of the South Oxfordshire Grim's Ditch having to negotiate much more uneven terrain). Unlike Aves Ditch, there is no known early Roman military base in the vicinity of the South Oxfordshire Grim's Ditch nor was the south in the aftermath of the Roman invasion the most likely direction from which to expect a threat. It thus seems most unlikely that the South Oxfordshire Grim's Ditch is a Roman military installation; on the premise that the similarities to

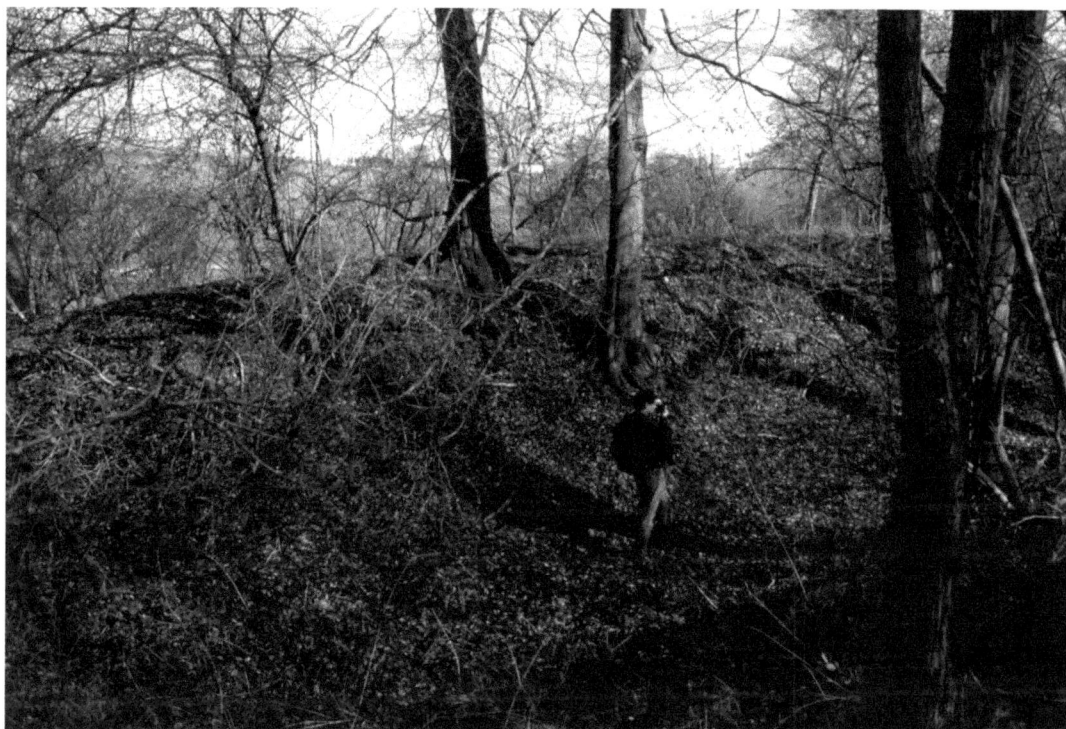

Figure 26. The South Oxfordshire Grim's Ditch may be the closest parallel to Aves Ditch, being of similar profile (even if in some sections more massive) and of similar straight alignment (even if not quite as straight as Aves Ditch, but running across much more uneven terrain).

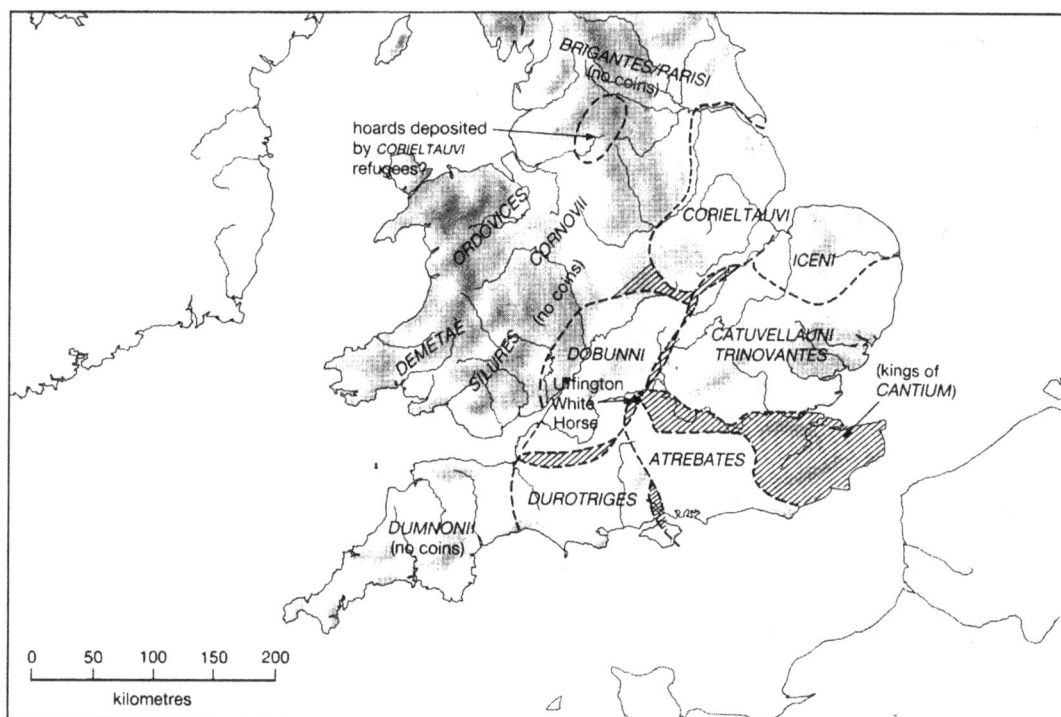

Figure 27. Approximate extent of territories controlled by coin-producing tribal groups in Britain, according to Barri Jones and David Mattingly. Hatching indicates where possession may have been in dispute or where it may have shifted. Interestingly, the postulated south-western extent of the tribal territory of the jointly ruled Catuvel-launi and Trinovantes, identified mainly on the basis of coin distribution and without taking into account the course of any linear earthworks, coincides strikingly with the location of Aves Ditch and the South Oxfordshire Grim's Ditch. Reproduced from Jones and Mattingly 1990: 55 map 3:12 with the kind permission of Professor David Mattingly.

Aves Ditch in date, profile and straight alignment, over a considerable distance, are too close to render it likely that they are coincidental, the same ought to be true for Aves Ditch.

These two linear monuments are, furthermore, roughly at the edges or intersection of the distribution zones of Catuvellaunian and Atrebatic and Catuvellaunian and Dobunnic coins respectively (**fig. 27**; Sellwood 1984; Cunliffe 1981: 37-9; Allen 2000: 27-32, esp. fig. 1.15). As many of these coins carry political messages, such as the names of tribal rulers (Van Arsdell 1989), and as there is not much overlap between the main finds concentrations of contemporary pieces attributed to different tribes, it seems reasonable to postulate that such coins circulated mainly within the territory of the relevant tribe or tribal confederation. Already Rivet (1958: 133-4, 146, 161 fig. 6), later Hodder (1977: 320-39, esp. fig. 66) and other scholars, as discussed below, placed the tribal boundaries in the vicinity of these two earthworks (without referring to them) on the basis of coin distribution and a postulated cluster of temples (such as Woodeaton) at the margins of tribal communities or the Roman *civitates* (administrative units) which succeeded them. The question thus arises whether the South Oxfordshire Grim's Ditch and Aves Ditch may indeed have marked the Catuvellaunian tribal boundary. The ditch is, from a Catuvellaunian perspective in both cases on the outside and the bank on the inside. That the South Oxfordshire Grim's Ditch may have formed the southern boundary of the Catuvellauni has been claimed independently by George Lambrick (1998: 12) and myself (Sauer 1998: 74-5) in 1998. Already John Hinchliffe (1976: 135) was convinced that 'It is surely a tribal boundary', even if he was cautious and avoided attributing it to any particular tribe, arguing instead that the identity of the ditch builders could only be a matter for speculation. That the earthwork functioned as a tribal boundary (without specification of the tribes) has also been considered as one option beside others by Neil Curtis (1994: 100).

It is interesting to note that recent research has traced a probable eastwards continuation of the South Oxfordshire Grim's Ditch (Ray 1991; cf. Potts 1907: 339-42) raising the possibility that (contrary to Bradley's [1969: 2-7] views) it was indeed intended to form a continuous boundary across the loop of the Thames between modern Wallingford and Henley-on-Thames; gaps may have been filled with hedges or other impenetrable vegetation. It is important here to stress that this is again roughly where the boundary between the Atrebates and the Catuvellauni was thought to have been already before the possible significance of the South Oxfordshire Grim's Ditch had been recognised (**fig. 27**; Jones and Mattingly 1990: 55 map 3:12; cf. 51; cf. Cunliffe 1991: 203 fig. 10.2 = 2005: 224 fig. 10.2). While we ought to bear in mind that coins and literary evidence suggest that the Atrebates neither formed a centralistic and permanently unified state, nor that that they had a stable border in the north (cf. Cass. Dio 60,19,1; Wacher 1995: 255, 257 fig. 116), Verica's temporary control of nearby Calleva (Silchester) (Bean 2000: esp. 204-5, 209), some time during the reign of Tiberius (AD 14-37), and the distribution pattern of his coins and that of his neighbours leave little doubt that the frontier with the Catuvellauni at the time has to be sought in the vicinity of the Thames in this region.

Equally Aves Ditch is in the immediate vicinity of the river Cherwell which was previously almost universally considered to form the boundary in the area (Rivet 1958: 146, 161 fig. 6; Salway 1981: 59-60; Sellwood 1984b: esp. 194-8; Branigan 1985: 27-8; Peddie 1987: 127; Cunliffe 1991: 171 fig. 8.10, 174; Blair 1994: xviii; Allen 2000: 27-32) and within Van Arsdell's postulated exchange zone between Dobunnic and Catuvellaunian territory (Van Arsdell and De Jersey 1994: 24-6 with map 19). Needless to say that coin distribution (cf. Allen 2000: 31 map 1.15) does not allow us to decide whether the natural or artificial landscape feature, in such close proximity to each other, formed the boundary, and it is anyway not necessarily a question of either or. If Aves Ditch formed an artificial line of control, then we need not assume that one entered Dobunnic territory as soon as one had crossed it; there may well have been a no man's land or a zone of exchange, of disputed possession or under some form of indirect control, beyond it (cf. Van Arsdell and De Jersey 1994: 23-5), even if nowhere as extensive as Caesar's (*B. Gall.* 6,23) clichéd image of the vast areas of no man's land around the territory of aggressive Germanic tribes. It is also worth noting that the Cherwell is meandering in the area and any movements across the long winding valley would have been hard to control effectively, whereas Aves Ditch is running over comparatively level ground (cf. **fig. 1**); it would have been ideally suited to prevent any unauthorised west-east traffic or to keep it under surveillance. In contrast to Tim Allen (2000: 29), I thus find it not difficult to reconcile the monument's proximity to the river with a potential boundary function.

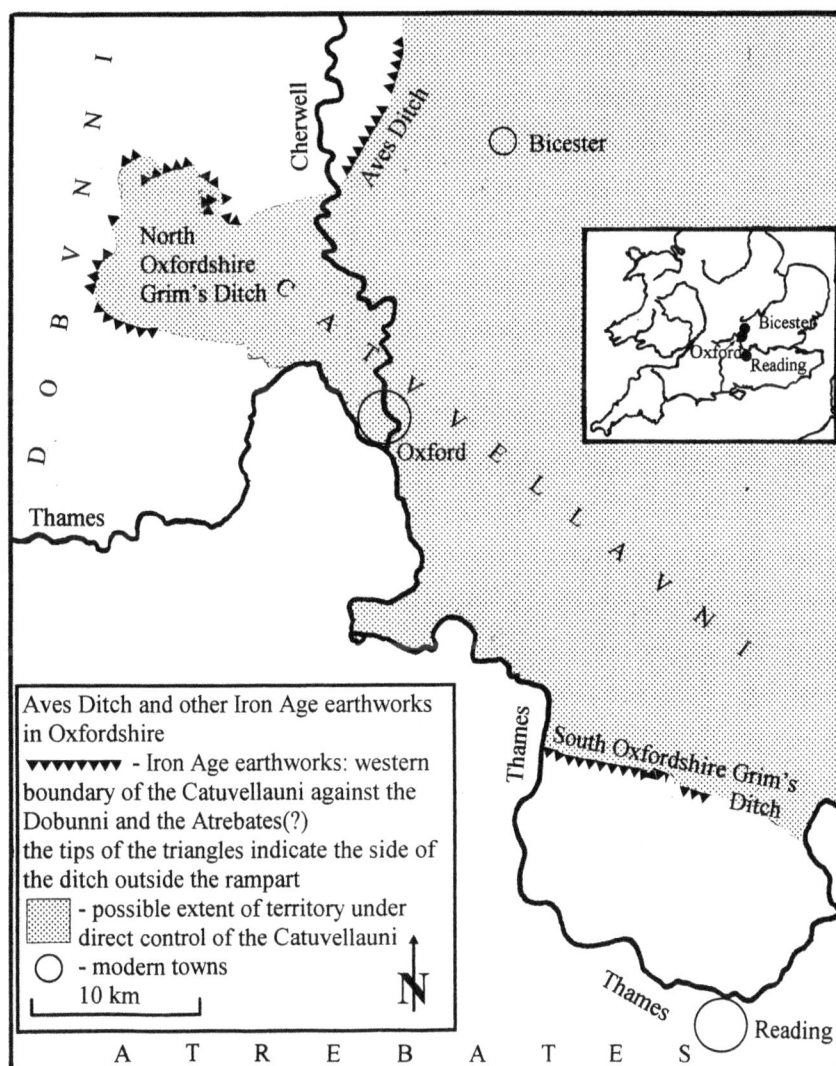

Figure 28. Hypothetical model of the possible function of Aves Ditch, the South and the North Oxfordshire Grim's Ditches as artificial boundary markers of territory under direct Catuvellaunian control.

That the two most monumental late Iron Age linear earthworks in the area (i.e. the South Oxfordshire Grim's Ditch and Aves Ditch) were both located in a boundary zone and constructed precisely at the time we know that this boundary zone existed, and that they are, furthermore, both of similar appearance and with the ditch facing away from Catuvellaunian territory (**fig. 28**) is unlikely to be mere coincidence, a theory (Sauer 1998: 74-5; 1999b; 1999c: 59-60; 1999d: 68) which has also been largely accepted by Allen (2000: 28-9). Barry Cunliffe (2005: 192) equally considers it possible that Aves Ditch demarcated a tribal boundary and that the location of the North Oxfordshire Grim's Ditch 'is suggestive of a border function'.

Much of the Catuvellaunian boundary between Aves Ditch and the South Oxfordshire Grim's Ditch will have been formed by the Thames, a river frontier which would have been easier to monitor than the meandering Cherwell north of Tackley. The theory that the Thames in this area indeed divided the territory of tribal communities gains strength in the light of the re-markable concentration of large late Iron Age *oppida* or 'valley forts' along this stretch of the river: Cassington, Abingdon and Dyke Hills (Lambrick 1998; Miles 1998: 16-17; Sauer 1999d: 68; Allen 2000: 29-31; cf. Sutton 1968). Tim Copeland (*pers. comm.*; cf. Copeland 2002: 70) kindly drew my attention to a potential additional valley fort in a meander of the Cherwell north of Enslow with a, as yet undated, double ditch in the north-west visible on aerial photographs (RAF photo, July 1949, SP 42/41 N.E.) which, whether deliberately placed in this position or mere coincidence, lies in approximate continuation of Aves Ditch and has roughly the same northing as the closest stretch of the North Oxfordshire Grim's Ditch west of the river Glyme. The size and lowland location of the (other?) valley forts on a major wa-terway (the Thames), notwithstanding the substantial defences, may point to a prosperous zone of exchange, which probably enjoyed at least longer episodes of peace or was under the protective umbrella of the hegemonic power (the Catuvellauni?), rather than one ravaged by permanent intertribal warfare. The archaeological evidence is indicative of a period of stable (natural and artificial) lines of control, but there is nothing to suggest that the Catuvellauni or the confederation of the Catuvellauni and Trinovantes (cf. De Jersey 2001) were constantly expanding their territory in a westwards and southwards direction, even if they appear to have done so in the years immediately before AD 43 (Cass. Dio 60,19,1; 60,20,2; Bean 2000: 209).

More contentious is what, if any, role the North Oxfordshire Grim's Ditch played in the sys-tem (**fig. 28**). One of the earliest assessments is provided by Warton (1783: 54-5) who exam-ined it on the ground with Mr Price of the Bodleian Library and preferred an interpretation as a boundary to that as a road and thought it definitely was not Roman; 'perhaps too rude even to be a Saxon work', he considered it to be a 'British against British' boundary. Warton was right in his dating proposal; the North Oxfordshire Grim's Ditch indeed appears to be a late Iron Age installation (Harden 1937). Whether or not he was right in postulating that it func-tioned as a boundary is in dispute. It is roughly contemporary to the two linear earthworks under discussion here and in my view, contrary to Copeland (2002: 65), similar to Aves Ditch in construction, overall width and height differential between the bottom of the ditch and the top of the bank (notwithstanding the considerable variations from section to section as pointed out above). Yet, in complete contrast to them, it does not form a straight line, but an extensive irregular bow. By some, it is thought to be a territorial *oppidum* (i.e. a proto-urban settlement with large tracks of the surrounding land being enclosed by earthworks) and, if so, one of the largest in Britain, covering an area of c. 80 km^2. While its potential defensive military func-tion dominated discussion in the past (e.g. Crawford 1930: 306 with references; Harding 1972: 58-60; 1974: 74-5, 225), more recently scholars prefer to see it as a possible area of special significance for gatherings, trade etc. (e.g. Copeland 2002: 63-9, 77-8). It is normally considered to be located within Dobunnic territory, a case recently supported by Allen (2000: 29; cf. 31 fig. 1.15) and Copeland (2002: 11) on the basis of coin distribution.

Yet, the problem remains that it would be odd for a territorial *oppidum* not to have a major known settlement anywhere in its interior (Miles 1986: 56). It is hard to see what evidence there is to suggest that in the early Roman period, this thinly populated stretch of land could have evolved into 'a centre of the client king's power' (Copeland 2002: 78), not to mention that the assignation of parts of the earthwork to the early Roman period is as hypothetical as the function. Furthermore, while it is appreciated that its eastern extent might have been marked by a section of the river Glyme (Allen 2000: 29), it still would be odd for a territorial *oppidum* of the Dobunni to be least well defined on the very side which is facing the nearby neighbouring tribe. A short-lived extension of Catuvellaunian territory to encompass a stretch of land, partially open and in agricultural use (cf. Copeland 2002: 43-70; Schumer 1999: 9-

12), is thus still perfectly within the realms of possibility and would relieve us from having to assume that one of Britain's largest territorial *oppida* is at the same time the one with the most minor traces of contemporary settlement in the interior. Tim Copeland (2002: 65), while coming to different conclusions, has put it aptly: 'Clearly, the Grim's Ditch took a great deal of effort to build, requiring more labour than can have come from the known settlement inside the dyke.'

Copeland (1989) was also able to demonstrate that the North Oxfordshire Grim's Ditch is far from being a single-phase and single-line installation. Yet, as Copeland acknowledges, since the phases are chronologically too close to be separable by associated artefacts, the phasing can only be proven where two stretches of the earthwork intersect, which appears to occur only at one point. Much of the phasing of the earthwork is thus necessarily conjectural, and there is nothing to disprove that much of the postulated phase 1 sections (the northern ones interestingly filling a large gap in the postulated phase 2 circuit) were upstanding at the same time as those thought to be of phase 2. Whether postulated phase 1 sections were deliberately, though not completely, filled in, let alone filled in before the construction of those attributed to phase 2, as Copeland (2002: 63; 1989: 279, 288-9), partially based on Harden (1937: 91) and Thomas (1958: 26, fig. 7), argues, is far from certain in my view. It hard to think of a sufficiently strong motive to fill many kilometres of ditch with heavy stones, unless this happened later to transform the banks into field boundaries and more level access routes to fields (see 'Aves Ditch in the Roman and post-Roman period'). It is worth noting here that parts of the North Oxfordshire Grim's Ditch served as a forest boundary in the Middle Ages (Salter 1908: 92-4 no. 649; cf. Ralegh Radford 1936: 24). Furthermore, one also should not underestimate the speed of natural erosion (Bell *et al.* 1996: esp. 234-6), especially for that period the bank was not colonised by a sufficient natural plant cover. A stony layer, similar in depth and compactness as in Copeland's phase 1 section of the North Oxfordshire Grim's Ditch and equally, undoubtedly, deriving from the bank, has also been observed at Aves Ditch in trench 1 (**fig. 16**) (and in the 1937 trenches [**fig. 23**], though less deep here, if the schematised drawings can be relied upon). Unless, we assume that Aves Ditch was deliberately dismantled as well, it seems more likely that we are dealing with the transformation of sections of the banks into tracks, and the resulting re-deposition of stones, and with erosion. Copeland is, however, certainly right that there are multiple lines of earthworks in some sections, probably representing an evolution of the system for added protection and, possibly, the marking out of a special zone within the loop-shaped monument, but we should be much more sceptical about the unproven and unlikely scenario of a large workforce dismantling the postulated earlier sections of one of the most extensive monuments of its kind in Britain.

Despite doubts concerning Copeland's theory of a small phase 1 being replaced by a large phase 2 circuit (with a postulated gap where phase 1 had been), there is no denial that the tentative explanation of the North Oxfordshire Grim's Ditch as a Catuvellaunian boundary marker is no more than a plausible hypothesis, and there are other possible interpretations. That Aves Ditch and the South Oxfordshire Grim's Ditch formed parts of an artificial tribal boundary, is, by contrast, not just a possibility, but, in my view, a fairly strong probability.

Despite erosion, no evidence appears to exist that the ditches of any of the earthworks were re-cut or cleaned out and the extracted material re-deposited on the bank, in contrast to the often complex history of earlier land divisions (e.g. Gosden and Lock 1998: 5-6, 8). This may add strength to the assumption that they were short-lived boundary earthworks. After the Roman conquest they would have become obsolete as defensible lines of control (but sections of them probably continued to be boundaries on an administrative level and in local memory). One might object, of course, that the assumption that hedges had been planted on the banks, or that the earthworks were symbolic more than practical installations, or that we are dealing (as far as Aves Ditch is concerned) with the quarry ditch for a road, could equally explain why it was never considered necessary to restore the, formerly deep and steep-sided, ditches to their original shape.

I ought to stress, however, that the theory that the Oxfordshire ditches formed tribal boundaries should not imply that we should visualise the Catuvellauni and Trinovantes as forming a centralistic state. It may be of significance that we find these boundaries concentrated in one area rather than more widespread around tribal territory (though it cannot be excluded that further earthworks elsewhere fulfilled a similar function, but have not yet been recognised as such). This observation, should the interpretation of these earthworks as probable boundary markers be accepted, may point to a local initiative by a subgroup of the tribe and the local aristocracy. Neither, however, should we exclude the possibility that there was central involvement in the decision to build them, in response to potential local problems in this particular boundary zone. Irrespective of whether the masterminds behind these linear barriers lived in the vicinity of their creations or in heartland of the Catuvellauni and Trinovantes, we must not overlook that the earthworks are at the likely boundaries with the Dobunni and the Atrebates, and have no known counterparts in the north and east. Unless the interpretation of the monuments as boundary markers is rejected, they thus offer support for some form of tribal unity, however tight or loose, as does the numismatic and literary evidence.

While the profile of Aves Ditch is by no means atypical for a prehistoric earthwork, its rectilinear alignment certainly is; if it is an Iron Age earthwork, then it is the straightest in Britain of this length which I am aware of. Some of the dykes attributed to the late Iron Age at Colchester and Chichester comprise long sections with a consistent alignment as well, though none includes a straight section of quite the same length as Aves Ditch (Hawkes and Crummy 1995 *passim*; Bradley 1971; Magilton 2003: 156-9, 167 no. 1). It is worth noting, of course, that both, the Colchester and Chichester dykes are associated with major centres, whereas Aves Ditch is in open terrain and not designed to protect and demarcate land around a central place of pre-Roman date. Of course, not only in the late Iron Age, but as early as the Neolithic there had been the ability to build remarkably straight so-called *cursus* monuments (i.e. probable ceremonial avenues), but the desire or ability (or both) to create dead-straight monuments had been lost in Britain long before the construction of Aves Ditch. While, as pointed out above, the idea of building an earthwork to mark a boundary could represent an indigenous tradition and need not go back to southern prototypes, the rectilinear orientation of Aves Ditch is much more likely to have been inspired by Roman installations. John Creighton (2000) has made a powerful case that, in the last century of pre-conquest south-east Britain (including the territory of the Catuvellauni), there was a strong aristocracy-led drive to imitate elements of Roman culture. These elements encompassed coin imagery, the evolution of proto-urban settlements, but also, occasionally, rectilinear architecture (Creighton 2000: 197-9, 205-13). Aves Ditch, as a monument presumably built on an aristocratic initiative (its construction requiring a large work force and control over an extensive stretch of land), may, despite its marginal position, be seen in a similar context.

ARTIFICIAL BARRIERS AT TRIBAL AND POLITICAL BOUNDARIES

Political and military explanations of archaeological remains, such as earthworks, are currently unfashionable (James 2003: 1-2), and recent scholars have sometimes concentrated on their symbolic significance (e.g. Darvill *et al.* 2002: 27). This is particularly true for prehistoric monuments where there is no direct written evidence to stand in the way of the preferred theoretical model. Simon James (*pers. comment*) has recognised this phenomenon and has coined the term the 'pacification of the past' to describe it. While there is no intention here to pre-empt his forthcoming work, nor any need to provide a survey of how this 'pacification of the past' has affected recent interpretations of prehistoric monuments, such as Iron Age hill forts, or prehistoric societies in general, it is necessary to explore briefly to what extent linear barriers could have had any real defensive capabilities. It is worth stressing that I have encountered myself 'pacifist' interpretations of the past, not just in print, but also in conversations with some fellow archaeologists. While the defensive value of relevant monuments is occasionally outright denied, much more frequently any evaluation of their potential military significance is simply omitted, be it out of disinterest or in the belief that they were never intended to be, or ineffective as, defensive installations. Yet, symbolism and real functional value as an artificial boundary control system are by no means mutually exclusive (Millett 1990: 139-41) and we should take scholarly advances on board without blindly following where fashion would lead us from one extreme to the other.

The recent preference for presenting us with a largely peaceful picture of the past may be closely linked to sub-sections of archaeology increasingly striving to emancipate themselves from text-based 'history' (Sauer 2004a). Yet, an assessment of the likelihood of late prehistoric linear earthworks functioning as political boundaries and, if so, how precisely it was envisaged that they should function to mark, control or defend those boundaries, would be severely impaired by disregarding ancient written testimonies. Even if these do not refer precisely to the community under investigation at precisely the right time, and even if they were written by authors living in core territories of the Roman world, rather than members of the tribal communities which had erected such earthworks, they still demonstrate (as we will see) some remarkable similarities over wide territories in the ways such earthworks functioned. Admittedly, ancient writers may well have overemphasised military aspects of linear barriers, at the expense of their potential symbolic or religious significance they may have been unaware of or uninterested in. Yet, even if the functional interpretations of ancient earthworks may often have been one-sided and incomplete, there is nothing to explain why classical authors would have described such barriers as being located at boundaries, if they were not – nor why they would have emphasised their defensive qualities, if they had none – nor why they would have stated that they were often erected in response to specific threats, if they were useless in counteracting such threats. No excuse thus is made or needed for discussing a range of textual references and possible archaeological parallels for linear earthworks, whose function may have been similar to that of Aves Ditch, even if none of them refers specifically to the Catuvellauni – or even to their neighbours.

There is, of course, no attempt here to present Aves Ditch, if its interpretation as a linear boundary is accepted, as a bulwark to bring major tribal attacks to a halt. Neither, however, would it be right to assume that it had no conceivable practical function and was a mere symbolic statement of the power of the community, which had erected it, or that it was meant as a way of expressing control by restricting movement of people across the landscape, in some undefined non-military way, to permitted routes. As far as Aves Ditch's postulated boundary function *per se* is concerned, it is worth stressing that the three longest and most substantial ancient linear barriers in Britain (even if they are all later), Hadrian's Wall, the Antonine Wall (**fig. 29**) and Offa's Dyke, all undoubtedly marked either a political boundary, or a line of

Figure 29. The Antonine Wall north-east of Bar Hill.

control in the hinterland of, but not far from, the edge of the territory under control, and the same is probably true for many other earthworks (Jankuhn 1976; Steuer 1999), such as possibly also the early medieval Wansdyke (Cunliffe 1993: 277, 294-6). The eighth-century Offa's Dyke was also similar to Aves Ditch in construction, even if the height differential between ditch bottom and bank tended to be higher and, of course, the earthwork was several times longer (Fox 1955; Hill and Worthington 2003).

The sections through Aves Ditch have established that it consisted of a substantial ditch with steep sides and a formidable stone bank (**figs 16 and 23**). As pointed out above (see 'The construction of Aves Ditch'), there is no conclusive evidence to suggest that Aves Ditch possessed a timber front or that it was reinforced with a palisade, but neither has enough of the earthwork been excavated to exclude either with certainty. Even if there never was more than a ditch and bank, reinforced, perhaps, with a hedge, it is worthwhile to look at analogies for similar installations in antiquity and how they were used. The closest parallel may be provided by a substantial *agger*, a Latin term describing an earth or stone rampart or causeway (which could equally have been used to describe the bank of Aves Ditch), which, according to Tacitus (Ann. 2,19-20), the Angrivarii in northern Germany had raised as an artificial boundary against the neighbouring tribe of the Cherusci, where this was not marked by natural obstacles. It was located in a forest clearing next to a river and a deep bog. Not only does Tacitus confirm that roughly at the same time (AD 16) a similar installation formed an artificial boundary elsewhere in north-west Europe, but we are even informed that this boundary rampart was used by Germanic tribesmen to take a stance against the attacking Roman army (*ibid.*). Furthermore, even Rome's professional soldiers had great difficulties in their attempts to storm it, while it provided the German defenders with an advantageous elevated position from where to inflict blows from above on the ascending soldiers. Only later, when employing long-range weapons, did the army succeed in driving the defenders off the rampart. Archaeological evidence suggests that the Germans also constructed a system of linear ramparts when laying an ambush for the Roman army at Kalkriese in AD 9 and that there was fighting along this line resulting in Roman losses (Schlüter 1999: 41-8). This need not mean that the *agger* of the Angrivarii or Aves Ditch were permanently garrisoned (they almost certainly were not), but they could have been used to await a hostile attack (if there was prior knowledge of it), while occupying higher ground. The postulated identification of the tribal boundary of the Angrivarii with a linear earthwork with timber revetment on its south side (i.e. the side thought to face the neighbouring Cherusci) at Leese in the 1920s (Bersu *et al.* 1926; Heimbs 1925) has been subject to much debate. While the uncertainty of the dating of this monument has been much emphasised, the identification still seems to be a possibility, though no more than that (Mildenberger 1978: 146); von Petrikovits 1967 (216-17 with no. 5; cf. Raddatz 1981: 122) tentatively dates it to the Middle Ages, but his evidence appears to be tenuous.

Worth noting is also the *lorica* and *vallum*, i.e. a bank reinforced with a palisade or breastwork (cf. Napoli 1997: 506; Rebuffat 1984: 11-12), which the Treveri in eastern Gaul built in the turbulent year AD 69 along their borders to help to defend themselves against Germanic incursions into their territory (Tac., *Hist.* 4,37; cf. 4,28). Whilst erected some 120 years after the annexation of their territory by Rome, it seems likely, in the absence of close Roman parallels of an earlier date, that the construction method and the location of the defences along their borders (*per fines suos*) reflect native tradition rather than foreign influence. Furthermore, it is worth stressing that, not only Tacitus's judgement, but also the historical context clearly suggests that the intended purpose was first and foremost military rather than symbolic or ritual.

In the event of surprise attacks such earthworks could have proven inconvenient for mounted raiders from the neighbouring community, especially if they had to be crossed by horses, captured livestock or any bulky booty. Caesar (*B. Gall.* 2,17) informs us that the Nervii in northern Gaul, because their cavalry was weak, protected their boundaries against mounted raids by their neighbours with impenetrable thorny hedges, consisting of bramble and thorn-bushes planted between an entanglement of numerous low branches of specially pruned and trained trees. There is no certain way to test whether or not Aves Ditch and the other linear earthworks in Oxfordshire were also provided with such a natural obstacle, whether or not as elaborate as that of the Nervii, but it is at least possible and it is worth noting that Mark Robinson's research (see below) suggests that there may have been a hedge running across or near trench 1 (even if its location and species remain a matter of speculation). The necessity for a raiding party to cut their way through hedges and to negotiate uneven ground would have made an escape (let alone a clandestine one) more difficult; it would have slowed down the retreat of such enemies, and increased the chances of them being caught and cornered on disadvantageous terrain by those defending the area.

The effectiveness of hedges as impenetrable barriers has equally been demonstrated by the creation of a hedge and other obstacles, some 1,500 miles long or more, as a customs barrier in India under British colonial rule in the nineteenth century. It was adapted to local terrain, vegetation and climate, and sections of it were grown on a raised bank (Moxham 2001: esp. 3, 102, 108, 194-7, 218-19 [reference kindly supplied by Chris Green and Patrick Erwin]; Sleeman 1893: 67-8 no. 3). While it should, of course, not necessarily be assumed that this nineteenth-century system in another time and climate zone, with different types of soil and ecosystems, possessed parallels in late Iron-Age Britain, its function and physical appearance probably provide a reasonably close analogy to the hedges of the Nervii. The latter predate Aves Ditch. Should hedges also have been employed as barriers in late Iron-Age Britain, then this could explain the discontinuous course of linear earthworks in boundary zones.

It is interesting to note that some archaeologists have reached similar conclusions as to the function of surviving ancient linear barriers, to that specifically attested for the Nervii by Caesar. Spratt (1982: 182) acknowledges that the multiple Scamridge and Oxmoor Dykes in

Yorkshire, the former also considered, possibly, to mark a tribal boundary (Spratt 1989: 14-20, 45-7), even though their dating is a matter of conjecture (cf. Spratt 1989: 11, 52), would have inhibited the rapid movement of animals or persons across them and would have been impenetrable, if thickly planted with hawthorn. Earthworks of more modest dimensions than the multiple earthworks in Yorkshire as well as hedges were still erected and used for purposes of border control and defence in late medieval Germany (Büttner 1998). That linear earthworks could be effective against cattle raiding has also been acknowledged for Irish examples by Ó Ríordáin (1979: 63-4) and is attested in a northern British context in St. Ethelred of Rievaulx's twelfth-century biography of St. Ninian (chapter 8; Pinkerton 1889: 28-9; cf. ix-xvii): thieves allegedly were induced to attempt to steal the late antique saint's cattle, as it was neither enclosed by a wall (*maceria*), nor a hedge or fence (*saepes*) nor a bank or rampart (*vallum*).

An interpretation as a tribal boundary, in this case between the Durotriges and Atrebates, has also been considered for the Bokerley Line/ Dyke (Darvill *et al.* 2002: 377), an earthwork system which appears to have been maintained into the post-Roman period, when it may have been made more defensive (Bowen 1990: 38-41). On the Continent, the c. 12 km long Olgerdiget in south-east Jutland (Neumann 1982, esp. 96; Jankuhn 1985) has equally been interpreted as a tribal boundary on the basis of the archaeological evidence. It consists of three or more lines of palisades (not all contemporary) in the west or north-west (extending over 7.5 km) and a ditch and rampart in east or south-east. Blocking an ancient trade route, it may have functioned as a toll barrier, an interpretation which is, of course, not mutually exclusive with that as a tribal boundary. The earthwork is split into various sections, which fill the gaps between natural barriers: a, now drained, lake and stretches of boggy terrain. In this instance, dendro-chronology provides a *terminus post quem* of AD 219 for its construction, so that, unlike the *agger* of the Angrivarii, we cannot exclude the possibility that it may have been influenced by the Roman 'Limes'. Interestingly, it is located precisely at the boundary of two of Jutland's four archaeologically defined regional groupings of the third and fourth centuries AD. The two cultural groupings on either side of the Olgerdiget appear to have evolved at about the same time as the barrier was constructed, suggesting that it may indeed have been erected by the southern group at the boundary with their northern neighbours (Christensen 2003; Neumann 1982). Slightly further south, the early medieval Danewerk (Stark 1988: 108-28, 177-83 with figs 1-3) is likely to have been erected for political and defensive purposes as well.

That linear barriers could be effective obstacles, rather than mere symbolic monuments, is also confirmed by other late examples, such as the highly effective late antique Claustra Alpium Iuliarum, consisting of a system of walls and fortifications (Šašel and Petru 1971; Ulbert 1981: 18-19, 42-9). The sheer scale of the late antique linear earthworks north of the middle and lower Danube (Kolník 1999; Soproni 1985: 11-17; Vaday 2002) also suggests, notwithstanding the ongoing debate on their precise dates of construction, that the massive investment of manpower promised to result in tangible benefits. That the late Roman long walls in Greece and the south-eastern Balkans, notably those across the Isthmus of Corinth (Gregory 1993) and in Thrace, were indeed effective in bringing several hostile incursions to a halt has been rightly stressed by Crow (1986). For similar reasons, namely in the belief that it would ensure his safety and preservation when hard pressed by the Huns, the ruler of the Gothic tribe of the Thervingi, Athanaricus, in AD 376 had fairly high walls built from the Siret (Gerasus) to the Danube, which interestingly from our perspective were touching or leading along the border with another Gothic tribe, the Taifali. This installation was considered to be effective (*efficax*) by the contemporary historian and military man Ammianus Marcellinus (31,3,7-8), notwithstanding the fact that the Huns, who did not await its completion, managed to spread panic, resulting in the flight of many Goths. Procopius (*Goth.* 4,26; *Pers.* 1,4; 2,4) equally provides a series of examples that linear ditches or walls could be highly effective against invaders. It is worth noting that in Late Antiquity such barriers were erected in frontier territory of smaller states or tribal communities, as well as, due to the frequent breakdown of borderline defence, across defensible isthmuses and mountain passes in the hinterland of the Roman Empire and its successor states. A Chinese source, referring to the fifth century AD, leaves no doubt that it was recognised in East and West alike that long walls and earthworks could significantly reduce the risk of hostile penetration and raiding beyond such barriers (Waldron 1990: 45).

Indeed, had linear earthworks and barriers as political boundaries been of purely symbolic significance, then it would be hard to explain why a high proportion of them, and even in cultures without contact with each other, follow the basic logic of defensive architecture. This is not only demonstrated by the massive scale of some of the installations, the depth of ditches and steepness of their sides, but, maybe more remarkably, by the frequency of the bank being on the inside of the territory to be demarcated or defended, the ditch being on the outside. In terms of the labour required or the symbolic significance, it would have made no difference whether the bank was build out of the spoil on the inside or the outside, and it would have saved time and efforts to construct a smaller bank on either side instead. Yet in terms of defensive capability, it made much more sense to construct a taller bank, rather than two smaller ones, as an elevated platform from where to expect an attack. It scarcely requires an explanation why it was advantageous to make enemies cross a ditch in front of it rather than offering them the opportunity to push the defenders back into a ditch behind their back.

It is necessary to re-emphasise that this need not mean that the banks were permanently manned, let alone along their entire length, only that relevant sections could be defended, if there was some advance warning. The above-quoted passage attesting that the Germans awaited the Roman attack from the top of such a linear earthwork suggests that the system at least occasionally worked. That not only in case of Aves Ditch and the South Oxfordshire Grim's Ditch, should the theory of them functioning as Catuvellaunian tribal boundaries be correct, but also in Africa's largest linear earthwork, the c. 1,000 year-old Sungbo's Eredo in south-west Nigeria (Darling 1997) and other west-African linear earthworks (Darling 1984: 85-7) the bank tends to be on the inside and the ditch on the outside is unlikely to be mere coincidence. The impression is unavoidable that, across the world, it was the norm rather than the exception, to take defensive considerations into account when constructing such installations. This impression is further strengthened by the observations that some earthworks can be shown to have led right to the edge of natural obstacles: swamps (in case of the Sungbo's Eredo [Darling 1998: 9-11], the *agger* of the Angrivarii and Olgerdiget) and forests (in case of the former two and probably many others, where it can no longer be proven as a result of our lack of knowledge of the precise extent of woods or scrubs in the period of construction of the relevant linear earthwork).

It ought to be stressed, of course, that real defensive capabilities and symbolic significance are by no means mutually exclusive; indeed, the former will always involve elements of the latter. Of course, linear boundary earthworks, being amongst the largest man-made landscape features of their time, would be seen as a symbolic statement of the power of the community who had constructed them, especially if the neighbour, they had been erected against, lacked the level of organisation necessary to create similarly monumental installations. They would probably have functioned like keep-out signs and visible reminders that any trespasser, crossing them, risked serious consequences, thus more often deterring unauthorised penetration into neighbouring territory than having their practical effectiveness being put to the test. That there could also be religious connotations (cf. Darling 1998: 9-10) in many cases, and that pit alignments and less elevated banks or more shallow ditches may have been primarily symbolic, is equally perfectly plausible, but that the most monumental earthworks were purely religious or symbolic monuments, without having any real and rational practical function, is not.

FROM AVES DITCH TO THE ANTONINE WALL?
THE EVOLUTION OF LINEAR BARRIERS IN THE ANCIENT WORLD

Whether or not all of the examples above are accepted, there is no doubt that artificial linear boundaries were a well-established phenomenon in the pre-Roman Iron Age in many regions in northern Europe. While there is no space here to discuss earlier prehistoric linear ditches (and other boundary markers, such as the distinctly non-defensive pit alignments [Thomas 2003]), it is worth stressing that there can be little doubt that the late Iron Age boundary earthworks were influenced by such earlier landmarks, notwithstanding the wide variety in physical appearance and, probably, function (cf. Ford 1981-82; Bradley *et al.* 1994).

Indeed, numerous linear ditches were already dug in the Bronze Age and early Iron Age, but the question of interest in our context is whether any of them already functioned as political boundaries. There is no space here to explore this question in any detail, and it ought to be stressed that, in absence of tribal coinage or written sources, it is impossible anyway to be certain whether archaeologically defined cultures correspond to political entities or whether or not some late Iron Age boundaries might reflect the course of much earlier ones. Two postulated artificial tribal boundaries in relative proximity to the ones discussed in this book nevertheless deserve to be mentioned. An interpretation as a tribal boundary has also been proposed for the Chiltern Grim's Ditch for an earlier phase of a postulated Catuvellaunian westward extension by Dyer (1963: esp. 49), though, in the light of the less precise chronology of the construction of this earthwork and our resulting lack of knowledge of contemporary tribal boundaries, this explanation has to remain purely hypothetical. More persuasive, even if ultimately unprovable as well, is Steve Ford's theory that the eighth to fifth century BC Berkshire Grims Ditch was 'a major socio/political boundary' on the basis of its length and location (Ford 1981-82: 1, cf. 17; 1983) and that, as in the case of Aves Ditch and the South Oxfordshire Grim's Ditch, there are few offshoot ditches and it does not enclose any tracts of land (Ford 1983: 35). It follows the eastern part of the northern escarpment of the Berkshire Downs; the absence in the west is explained by the more distinct escarpment and the presence of hillforts being sufficient to emphasise the boundary (Ford 1981-82: 17, partially based on Bradley, *pers. comm.*). It also seems to separate two eighth-century BC pottery style zones (Ford 1983: 36). In the west of the northern escarpment of the Downs, we also find the enigmatic Uffington White Horse (**fig. 30**), created between 1740 and 210 BC at 95.4% confidence level (Rees-Jones and Tite 2003). Barri Jones and David Mattingly (1990: 51) argue that it may have marked a point where the tribal territories of the Atrebates and Dobunni met (**fig. 27**). The monuments and associated finds in the surroundings certainly suggest that it continued to attract gatherings throughout the Iron Age and Roman period (Miles *et al.* 2003), even if this provides no ultimate proof that it was a boundary landmark. Whether or not the Berkshire Grims Ditch may have marked a political boundary already in the early Iron Age, there is little doubt that prehistoric earthworks would have influenced later monuments of this kind, such as the South Oxfordshire Grim's Ditch.

It equally seems likely that such visible landmarks would, to some extent, have inspired later Roman barriers, such as the Antonine Wall. Yet, we should avoid any monocausal explanation. Schuchhardt (1900: 99-103; 1931: 3-10) argued that the Roman linear defences were modelled on Germanic prototypes, while erroneously claiming (Schuchhardt 1931: 8) that there was no evidence for such pre-Roman linear earthworks in Britain. In von Petrikovits's (1967; cf. Crow 1986: 724-5) view, by contrast, pointing to the fifth-century BC long walls

Figure 30. The Uffington White Horse on the north slope of the Berkshire Downs, overlooking the plain.

Figure 31. The 'Limes' in the Roman province of Upper Germany in its most developed form with bank, ditch, palisade and stone watchtowers; reconstructed section at Zugmantel.

linking Athens and the Piraeus harbour and other examples, Roman linear defences have to be seen in Greek tradition.

Ball (2000: 312-17) favours a third alternative and postulates that Roman long walls and barriers appear to derive from eastern, i.e. Parthian, central Asian, Mesopotamian and/or eastern Mediterranean, tradition. There are, undoubtedly, many examples for such monuments in this area (Crow 1986: 724), even if the dating evidence for the most extensive and advanced example, the 190 km-long Sadd-i Iskandar with 33 associated forts south-east of the Caspian Sea, is by no means clear. Kiani (1982: 38) tentatively dated it to the reign of Mithridates II (123-87 BC), which seems perfectly possible. A lower sea-level of the Caspian Sea for much of the first millennium AD, which would probably have left an undefended gap between the western terminal of the wall and the coast, may equally point towards an earlier date, yet with less precision (Huff 1981). Nevertheless, the chronological indicators presented so far are insufficiently precise to exclude a later date for this long brick wall with certainty. It is, however, undoubtedly true that Sadd-i Iskandar in Iran, Hadrian's Wall, the Antonine Wall and the German 'Limes' (**fig. 31**), being associated with a chain of forts, represent more sophisticated lines of control than their prehistoric counterparts. South-west of Sadd-i Iskandar, and, like it, running from near the coast of the Caspian Sea (presumably from the ancient coast line) to the Elburz Mountains, we find the Wall of Tammīsha, built of similarly-sized large rectangular bricks. Whether or not this may indicate that the two walls might be contemporary and, if so, that the Wall of Tammīsha may have formed a second and shorter line of defence, is uncertain. Conventionally, the latter wall is thought to date to the sixth century AD (Bivar and Fehérvári 1966), and some still believe that Sadd-i Iskandar may be of late Parthian or Sasanian date as well (cf. Schottky 1998: 461-2, 468). The 15 km long so-called 'Median Wall', with brick stamps of the Neo-Babylonian king Nebuchadnezzar (605-562 BC), proves in any case that linear barriers also have a long tradition in the Near East (Killick 1984; Wilkinson 2003: 60), and there are other examples for early long walls in central and south-eastern Asia, some of them possibly functioning as boundaries (Ball 2000: 315).

In the north-west there are not just the British examples, but recent scientific dating has established that some of Ireland's linear earthworks, including the Black Pig's Dyke which may mark a political boundary as well, are significantly earlier than their Roman imperial counterparts (Waddell 1998: 358-60). Northern Africa represents yet another geographical area in the ancient world, from which a pre-Roman linear boundary is known: the Carthaginians marked the extent of their African territory with a ditch, though little is known about it (Gsell 1920a: 101-3; 1920b: 289-91; Lancel 1995: 262-3).

That there are early examples even further afield, attested in literature (Herodotus 4.12) or still extant (Ball 1982: 145 no. 520, 498 map 81; Rakhmanov 1994), hardly needs stressing. Most notably, the ancient Chinese barriers, equally predating their Roman equivalents, are worth noting. They formed not as unified a system as is commonly thought today, but were clearly built to mark or protect political boundaries. Some of the linear earthworks in China were even erected long before the creation of the famous defensive system of the third century BC (Waldron 1990: esp. 13-43). While much older than their Roman counterparts, it is hardly necessary to emphasise that, in the light of the limited mutual contacts (Ferguson 1978; Heimberg 1981), there is nothing at all to suggest that Roman linear defensive systems, let alone prehistoric banks and dykes, were in any way directly influenced by functionally similar installations in the Far East.

By contrast, it is highly probably that Roman linear barriers were to some extent inspired by north-west European examples, but there is noting to suggest that this was their main, let alone their sole, root. There are appears to have been some leeway for governors and military units in the physical execution of these border control systems (hence the German 'Limes' in its last phase consisting of a bank, ditch and palisade in Upper Germany (**fig. 31**) and of a wall in the adjacent province of Raetia). However, since the decision to build such major installations was taken at an imperial rather than at a provincial level, it would be hazardous to argue that the fact that they are much more frequent and extensive in the north-west than at any other frontier may be due in part to pre-Roman local traditions. The Roman and the Parthian (or Sasanian?) linear boundaries cluster both in areas where there was strong pressure from tribal societies rather than highly organised states against which they would have been of more limited value (an observation, incidentally, which argues against them having been pure boundary control installations) and where there were no suitable natural obstacles. Indeed, the Parthian (or Sasanian?) Sadd-i Iskandar with its string of forts is much closer to the Roman systems, but the plausible hypothesis that it is earlier still awaits confirmation (or correction). Even if the prototypes for Roman linear barriers cannot be traced back to a single geographical origin, Rome adopted the idea, as many other military innovations, almost certainly from societies integrated into the Empire as well as from its opponents, in east and west alike, rather than developing the concept of Roman linear frontiers in a vacuum.

AVES DITCH IN THE ROMAN AND POST-ROMAN PERIOD

The bottom of the ditch was in both, the 1937 and 1997/98 sections, filled with stones which must have eroded from the bank (**figs 16 and 23**). Modern experiments (Bell *et al.* 1996: esp. 234-6; cf. Fasham 1987: 67-78) have shown that ditches within less than a decade can silt up to the extent that steep sides are transformed into gentle slopes. A layer of re-deposited stones from the bank has also been observed in the North Oxfordshire Grim's Ditch (as pointed out above). Much of the massive stone banks of these two monuments, once they had lost their original function, would, as obstacles to agriculture or the movement of livestock, most likely have evolved into field boundaries and access routes to farmland. Such a transformation of sections of the earthworks into local tracks in the Roman period would probably have involved some artificial levelling of the top of the bank and the re-deposition of excess stones into the adjacent ditch. Even if there is no way to test this hypothesis, it seems likely that prior to this postulated re-use, the Aves Ditch bank would not have had such a level surface. The postulated secondary use of banks as local roads, used by humans, animal herds and carts, would in any case have entailed wear, destruction of vegetation and erosion. If the top of Aves Ditch functioned as a minor traffic route in the Roman period, as seems likely, then this would have made it in any case more difficult for vegetation to become established on the top, even if the slope to the ditch need not have been exposed to much wear. Roman pottery, probably of the later first to, possibly, second century from the re-deposited bank material in the ditch of Aves Ditch in trench 1 (**fig. 16**) adds strength to the assumption of a significant level of erosion occurring early in the Roman period. The postulated transformation of the earthwork from a tribal boundary marker to a road following a probable administrative boundary seems natural; not only would the stone bank have been hard to remove and unsuitable for cultivation, we also must assume that for a tribal boundary earthwork to be controllable, if needed, there must have been a track following it from the start (maybe on the inside of the bank).

The fact that Roman finds have been found fairly high in Aves Ditch, in all 1937 trenches (incl. a mid third to fourth-century sherd in trench III; **fig. 23**), suggests, incidentally, that sediment accumulation may have accelerated later in the Roman period, as far as this particular area is concerned. This possibly increased speed of erosion in the Roman period may be partially the result of the intensification of agriculture (cf. Robinson and Lambrick 1984: 813) and partially of the potential use of the bank as a track already in antiquity. The finds from trench 2 (**fig. 16**) four kilometres further north, however, remind us that some caution is required, in the light of the fact that at Aves Ditch, as at many other sites, few artefacts have been lost between the late Roman period and modern times; it is possible that some of the Roman artefacts are residual, and their deposition could post-date their production by centuries, even by more than a millennium. Had we missed a single glass fragment, the finds from trench 2 would form a neat stratigraphic sequence: the fill of the curving ditch and 0.60 m of deposits, which built up on top of it, contained otherwise exclusively Iron Age sherds. A Roman coin from the top of context 30, dating to c. AD 260-400, is in absolute and relative terms on a higher level than any of the Iron Age artefacts (**fig. 16**). Yet, the glass fragment, dated by Birgitta Hoffmann (below) to the sixth to eighth or the eighteenth century, indicates that the significant level of sediment accumulation (after the section of the curving ditch east of the bank of Aves Ditch had been filled up with stony material [contexts 36 and 35], probably deliberately when the linear monument was constructed), did not occur before Anglo-Saxon times at the earliest and, conceivably, not until modern times. It ought to be stressed, however, that this is of no direct relevance to the dating of the bank of Aves Ditch, since there is no evidence to suggest that any of these deposits are stratigraphically older than the bank. Indeed, our assumption must be that the tail of the bank (to be sought in the unexcavated gap between trenches 1 and 2) is overlain by these horizontal medieval or modern deposits while mid Iron Age pottery embedded in them appears to be re-deposited.

As far as trench 1 is concerned, we are on firmer ground. The radiocarbon date leaves no doubt that the depth of the ditch fill, when the grave was cut in the late seventh, eighth or, possibly, ninth century, was about halfway between the rock-cut bottom of the ditch and the modern surface. The depth of modern finds in context 7 (**fig. 16**), indicates that there appears to have been hardly any erosion between the early Middle Ages and modern times, as indicated by the depth of post-medieval artefacts in the ditch fill. This apparently low level of erosion may be related to heath land being in the area of the trench in the early nineteenth century and probably before. In the eighteenth century a lime kiln (Davis 1797) and an associated quarry, both still visible today (**figs 6 and 7**), appear to have been established near our trenches. Fortunately, the abandoned limestone quarry never reached the vicinity or destroyed any part of Aves Ditch. The recent past saw also, unsurprisingly, an accelerated rate of erosion in the ditch. The fill (context 6A) of the modern re-cut (context 44) within the ditch, which may be associated with the parish boundary, was rich in modern artefacts, ranging from glass (including large parts of chunky bottles of antique appearance) to china and metal objects.

Two sets of undated, c. 6 cm wide wheel ruts (contexts 49A-D), caused by wagons with a wheelbase of c. 1.55 m (centre to centre), just over five English feet, on the top of the Aves Ditch bank in trench 1, are likely to be modern, partially because this is wider than the wheelbase of Roman wagons, at least as observed from wheel ruts in the Alps (Pöll 2002: 76-7), more importantly because they are filled with topsoil (context 1). The stones at the bottom of these ruts showed wear on the surface. Less distinct remains of probable modern cart tracks (contexts 50A-D) were also observed to the west of the ditch (within trench 1). Prior to the planting of trees in the Gorse and the modern encroachment of scrub onto the bank, wheeled traffic seems to have followed the landmark, using both, the top of the bank as well as a strip of land to the west of the ditch. This traffic may in part have been responsible for the accelerated erosion affecting Aves Ditch in modern times.

THE BEHEADED SKELETON

Burials in re-used ancient earthworks are by no means uncommon. Lieutenant-General Pitt-Rivers (1892: esp. 214-15), for example, found three skeletons in one of his sections through the fore dyke of the Bokerley Dyke, all buried there long after the construction of this earth-work, once the ditch had silted up to a significant extent. Four, so far undated, burials were found in a small section through the South Oxfordshire Grim's Ditch, three of them in the bank and one on the lip of the ditch (Hinchliffe 1976: 125-8). Other examples for burials in reused ditches are too numerous to list here. Ritual as well as pragmatic reasons may have motivated such secondary use. As far as the latter are concerned, it may not be without inter-est that, on information by a local resident, it used to be difficult to dig grave pits in the adja-cent parish with the telling name Middleton Stoney, owing to the hard limestone bedrock. The suffix 'Stoney' of Middleton Stoney, first attested in 1552, may refer to the stoniness of the ground (Gelling 1953: 228-9). A burial in the ditch of the earthwork (**fig. 32**) would have saved labour, when disposing of an unwanted body, while avoiding the health hazard and the stench its decomposition above ground would have caused.

Figure 32. The burial in the ditch with the upper body and the feet *in situ* seen from south-west on 4 June 1998; the bank is in the back-ground. Each segment of the scales (excl. the pointed tips) measures 500 mm.

While it thus could be ar-gued that we should have been prepared for the pos-sibility that we might en-counter human remains in the ditch, the discovery of a burial in trench 1 still came as a great surprise. It was first encountered in autumn 1997 when a nar-row trench (no. 1) was dug through the earthwork. The use of mattocks to excavate the ditch fill (necessary as the lower ditch fill was too stony for the effective use of trow-els within the time avail-able in autumn 1997) re-sulted, unfortunately, in the dislocation of most leg bones, except for the feet, and much of the right hand, before it was no-ticed that these were bones in anatomical context. Having recognised this, we were then immediately able to recover a high pro-portion of the bones and to record the precise location of some bone material, which had remained *in situ*. The three-dimensional position of

Figure 33. The burial under excavation on 4 June 1998.

these bones enabled us later to reconstruct the orientation of the burial and to predict precisely which parts of the anatomy were to be expected beyond either profile and at what precise height above sea-level. The trench was thus re-excavated and extended in spring 1998 with the aim of recovering the remainder of the burial. Being aware of the precise depth of the skeleton and in the expectation that we would encounter the top of the skull well above the remainder of the bones, we used only trowels and finer tools from over a foot above the re-corded remains downwards (**fig. 33**). To our surprise, we did not find a skull, but uncovered no more than a small skull fragment from the cranial vault (see Hacking below), 30 cm west of the closest edge of the lower jaw and, at 107.79 m above sea-level, i.e. 21 cm above the highest point of the jaw. We also found an isolated human tooth, a lower incisor (identified by Peter Hacking), 14 cm to the east of the closest edge of the lower jaw and, at 107.705 m above sea-level, 12.5 cm higher than the highest point of the jaw. We did not succeed in find-ing the remainder of the skull, except for the above-mentioned lower jaw which, whilst being fragmented (possibly when much of the remainder of the skull was dug out, or, more proba-bly, later as a result of the weight of the stones above it [Peter Hacking, *pers. comm.*]), was still in the area and vicinity of its correct anatomical position; the lower six of the neck verte-brae were all still *in situ* (**figs 34 and 35**). It hardly needs stressing that the excavation team working carefully and slowly with trowels and leaf tools could not have missed any bones, let alone an almost complete skull, had it been there. The remainder of the skeleton of what proved to be a c. 35-year old man (see Hacking below) was, except for some minor tree root interference and the sternum being found 7 cm on the right/ east side of the centre of the spi-nal column, between the ribs, undisturbed.

The stratigraphy was difficult; the grave cut could only be discerned tentatively (and for a while we had even considered the possibility that the body had been placed on the bottom of the ditch and covered with a pile of stones and soil), but this need not be a surprise. The grave was cut into re-deposited loose stony rampart material and appears to have been filled with

Figure 34. The upper body of the skeleton on 4 June 1998: note that the bottom is disturbed by the 1997 trench, while no modern disturbance, other than tree roots, affected the remainder of the skeleton. Most of the skull had been removed in antiquity.

Figure 35. The first thoracic, the seventh to fifth neck vertebrae and parts of the lower jaw *in situ* after further cleaning (and exhumation of the clavicles), and prior to en-bloc recovery, on 7 June 1998. Note that the fifth neck vertebra is in a higher position than the visible fragment of the lower jaw. The fourth, the damaged third and the undamaged second neck vertebrae are not visible on the picture, but were recovered.

spoil of precisely the same origin. The left/ western ulna was lying on a stone and therefore its lower/ northern parts were positioned 60 - 80 mm higher than the radius and the hand. It was also broken, probably under the weight of the fill of the grave pit. This suggests that the bottom of the grave pit was stony and uneven and that the weight of the stony fill, piled on top of the body, resulted eventually in these dislocations after death. The postulated collapse of the fill of the grave pit after the disintegration of the soft tissue may also explain why the sternum had been knocked out off its proper anatomical position and how a stone got wedged between two of the lumbar vertebrae. No obvious gnaw marks were observed on any of the bones (Peter Hacking, *pers. comm.*). Animals, eating the flesh, particularly in the cold season, can leave such marks on the bones, if a body is left lying on the surface (Berg *et al.* 1981: 107-8). The absence of gnaw marks, in conjunction with the fact that the bones were in perfect anatomical order, disregarding tree-root action, and that nothing in the areas excavated in 1998 was missing, other than most of the skull, suggests that the body had been buried beyond the reach of scavengers. This must equally be true of the skull, as its fragmentation *in situ* can hardly be explained by animal interference. We can be sure that the man had not been beheaded prior to his burial. If the head had been cut off prior to advanced decomposition, it could not have been removed without the lower jaw and the upper neck vertebrae. Only after much of the soft tissue had decomposed could the lower jaw, accidentally or deliberately, be separated from the remainder the skull. (There is no evidence for the use of cutting implements.) It is equally hard to imagine how that fragment of the cranial vault would have broken off and could have been left behind, whilst still held in place by soft tissue. The neck vertebrae provided another clue to the gruesome procedures the mortal remains of the deceased had been subjected to some 1,200 to 1,300 years ago: while the remainder of them were in their correct anatomical position, the atlas was not found and thus probably removed together with much of the skull. We can thus infer that some soft tissue, attaching this uppermost neck vertebra to the base of the skull, still survived when the body was dismembered. Soft tissue is thought to completely decompose within about seven years of the death of an individual in case of a burial (and two years if the body is left unburied [Berg *et al.* 1981: 108]).

Having ruled out other options, this leads to the surprising, but inevitable conclusion that the intact body of the deceased was buried, allowed to decompose below ground and that only at a later date, but probably within a few years of the burial, one or more grave intruder(s) dug down to the burial, damaged the skull, removed most of it, but overlooked a fragment which had broken off. No attempt was made then to recover any of the remainder of the skeleton or even the lower jaw. It seems highly unlikely that this happened coincidentally as a result of potential earthmoving operations for a different purpose, especially since there is no evidence that the ditch was ever re-cut. (Unlike a grave cut filled up immediately with the extracted material, a re-cut of the ditch would almost certainly have been easy to spot; if left open, rain water would have washed in finer sediments, which would have been easy to distinguish from the stony matrix of contexts 8B and 9D.) Furthermore, had the skull been removed accidentally in the course of a purely hypothetical and otherwise unrecognised re-cutting of the ditch, then it would have been more likely (even if not certain) for the isolated tooth and the skull fragment to have been dislocated in the direction of the ditch, i.e. to the south or to the north; they were, however, found to the west and to the east of the jaw (i.e. at a right angle to the likely working direction and against the gradient of the ditch). The archaeological evidence offers thus strong support for a targeted intervention (and probably a ritual act) rather than an accidental removal.

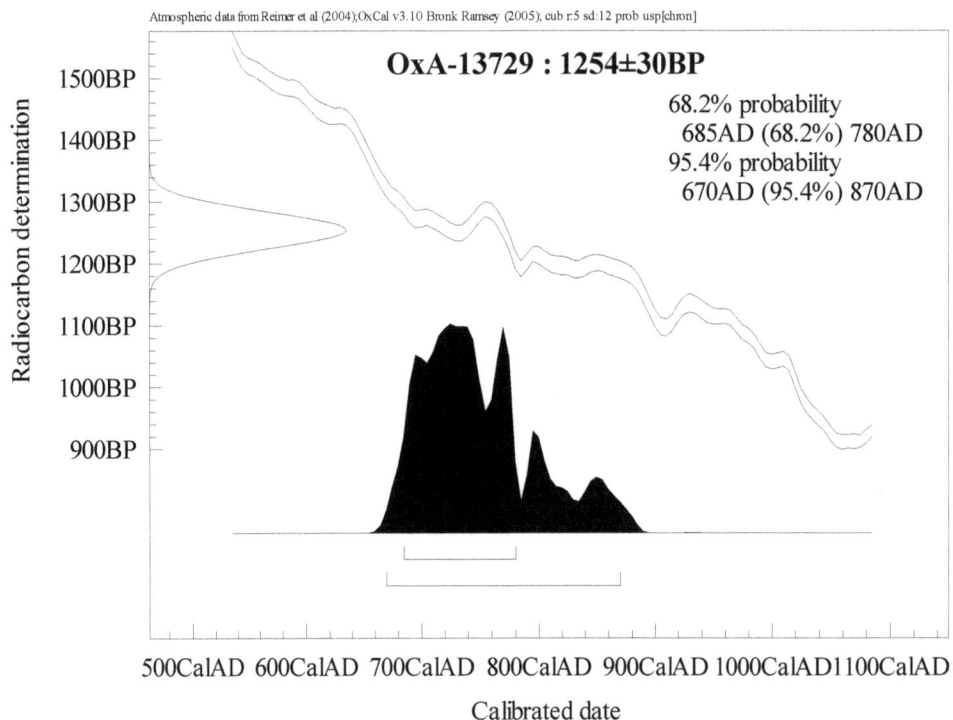

Figure 36. The radiocarbon sample from the right radius of the human skeleton from context 8C (OxA-13729: 1254±30 BP) kindly provided by Dr Tom Higham (RLAHA, University of Oxford).

Crucial for the correct interpretation of this macabre intervention is, of course, its date. It was clear that none of the pottery sherds found within the grave need have been deliberately put or accidentally lost there at the time of its creation, but all could have been, and probably were, re-deposited. The fact that only isolated single sherds, and no remains of complete vessels or other items were found, not to mention that none of the small number of pieces was contemporary to the burial, excludes the possibility that we are dealing with grave goods. (And the same appears to be true for the few random animal bones found in the grave [see Knight below].) The latest sherd provides a later first-century *terminus post quem* for the grave. A radiocarbon sample from the right radius of the skeleton confirmed that this *terminus post quem* was correct, but predated the death of the male individual by over half a millennium. He died between AD 685 and 780 (with a probability of 68.2%), or between AD 670 and 870 (with 95.4% certainty) (**fig. 36**; see 'The date of Aves Ditch').

Archaeomagnetic samples from the bottom of context 7 (see Erwin below with **fig. 41**), by contrast indicate that this deposit began to build up c. AD 275-550. This is surprising, as stratigraphy suggests strongly that context 7 post-dates the grave cut (45 and, of course, its fill, 8C), while the latest possible archaeomagnetic date for the beginning of its formation is over one century earlier than the earliest possible carbon-14 date for the skeleton. It ought to be stressed, however, that the archaeomagnetic samples, whilst plotted in **fig. 16** on the same section as the grave cut, were all taken, after the burial had been exhumed, from the trench 1 1998 north and south profiles, either of which was beyond the probable extent of the grave cut (cf. **fig. 13**). In the light of the, apparently, extremely slow sedimentation rate in the post-Roman period (see 'Aves Ditch in the Roman period'), the surface level in the ditch is unlikely to have risen by more than a few centimetres in the course of the early Middle Ages, and, with the benefit of hindsight, the archaeomagnetic samples should have been taken above the grave cut and before exhumation of the skeleton. The differences in level between the fifth/ sixth century and the seventh/ eighth century were probably so minute that the question arises whether the grave may have been cut from, in relative terms, a marginally higher level (the very bottom of context 7 being destroyed in this area), or whether the archaeomagnetic dating may be less reliable than the radiocarbon dating. However, it is worth noting that the grave with its stony fill was at no stage visible in plan and has only been tentatively identified in section, mainly on the basis of a higher concentration of stones towards the top of the postulated fill of the grave (8C) in comparison with the adjacent deposits, 8A and 8B; this would suggest that it was indeed cut from a level below context 7. Further indications for the location of the grave cut are offered by what appeared to be an almost vertical edge between contexts 8C and 8B. Furthermore, the regular band of stones separating context 7 from contexts 8A, B and C equally suggests that this band marks where the bottom of the ditch had been for some time and that the grave was probably cut from this surface. It thus appears probable that context 7 in its entirety postdates the grave cut, in which case the archaeomagnetic dates are too early.

BURIAL IN THE DITCH AND BEHEADING: ATTEMPT AT AN EXPLANATION

Various forms of special ritual treatment of the human head, in particular the use of head trophies (often of enemies), has, as is well known, a long tradition in virtually all parts of the world, and in some up to the recent past (e.g. Jacobs 1990: esp. 116-29). While there is no space here to discuss the phenomenon of head trophies in detail, it is worth noting in our context that there is copious evidence from Iron Age north-west Europe (e.g. Diod. Sic. 5,29,4; Benoit 1981: 23-4, 53-99; Cunliffe 1991: 506-8, 519; Boylston *et al.* 2000: 249-53). Whether or not there is any connection with this pre-Roman ritual, we encounter another form of ritual beheading in late Roman Britain. Decapitated burials are so frequent in Britain in this period that there can be little doubt that we are dealing predominantly with a *post-mortem* ritual act rather than an application of this particular form of capital punishment on an unprecedented scale (Philpott 1991: 77-89, 440-1 fig. 23; cf. Booth 2002: 24, 26-7 tab. 2). No less than four amongst 31 documented inhumations, for example, unearthed in the vicinity of the town of Alchester (just c. 7 km from Aves Ditch) and certain or presumed to date to the late Roman period, had been decapitated and the head invariably placed near the feet (Booth *et al.* 2002: 152-61; Boyle 2002: 385-8; Sauer 2004c: 83). Decapitation shortly after death appears to have been the norm (cf. Watt 1979; MacDonald 1979: 415), but occasionally the body must have been allowed to decompose before complete bones could be removed and repositioned (Crawford 1982: 40-2) as happened also in the case of the skull of the Aves Ditch man. The practice was, self-evidently, ritual in nature, an argument further strengthened by the burial of babies in the corners of temple IV at Springhead, two of them decapitated and of a beheaded gull nearby (Boon 1976: 171-2 with fig. 5; Penn 1961: 121-2; 1965: 177). In contrast, the absence of decapitated burials in larger late Roman and post-Roman cemeteries is a possible indicator for a Christian burial ground (Rahtz *et al.* 2000: 411, 419-20). The pagan practice of *post-mortem* beheading continued, nevertheless, into the post-Roman and Anglo-Saxon period though the general impression remains that it decreased in frequency (O'Brien 1999 *passim*; cf. Harman *et al.* 1981: 166; Clarke 1979: 374-5); Elizabeth O'Brien's research indicates that decapitation of burials in the early Middle Ages is indeed likely to be a survival of an indigenous tradition and she even argues that the continued application of *post-mortem* beheading in the upper Thames valley area may indicate 'some sort of stability of population in the region during the transition period' (O'Brien 1999: 174). *Post-mortem* decapitation is also attested on the Continent in the Merovingian period and Simmer (1982) advances the theory that the ritual, equally thought to be rooted in the pagan past, is a precursor of the later separation of skulls from the other human bones in charnel houses. It might be going too far to examine here the separation of the skull from the body in the context of the Christian veneration of the relics of martyrs (e.g. Angenendt 1991: 333), or recent folklore, such as the ghostly rides of a headless hunter in a wood with two Roman villas in southern Germany (Paret 1932: 256; Binder 1924: 121), or to postulate that there are coherent links between the myriad of rituals and religious beliefs involving decapitation or head trophies all over the ancient and even the New World (e.g. Haberland 1991: 210-11, 224-6). Yet, it is clear that numerous religious rituals centred on the human head evolved all over the world and sometimes in similar forms even in genuinely unrelated cultures. In order to try to reveal what underpinned the ritual observed at Aves Ditch a slightly more narrow focus is required.

One of the keys to understanding why the Anglo-Saxon Aves Ditch skeleton was subjected to *post-mortem* beheading may be its location. Andrew Reynolds (1997; 1998: 8; 2002: 175-81, 187-8; cf. Pitts 2002: 141-2; Semple 1998: 113, 121) has demonstrated that places of execution and burial sites of executed criminals, sometimes called 'heathen burials', were often located at boundaries of Domesday hundreds or estates; such individuals were denied burial in consecrated ground (Reynolds 1997: 37-9; 2002: 179; Thompson 2002: 233) while the boundary of this unit of local government and jurisdiction seemed an appropriate place to dispose of their mortal remains without undue efforts. For much of the second millennium all of Aves Ditch was within the Ploughley hundred, whose nearest boundary was formed by the river Cherwell (Lobel 1959: xxviii), just 2.6 km from the 1997/98 trenches. However, prior to 1086 Northbrook was part of a First Gadre hundred, whose precise extent is unknown (*Domesday Book 14, Oxfordshire*: 29,20; Morley Davies 1947-52: 236-7; Lobel 1959: 2), and of the Woodstock rural deanery (Morley Davies 1947-52: 240). Thus it seems possible that Aves Ditch could have formed a hundred boundary in the Anglo-Saxon period. Interestingly, Philip Tallon (1999) has observed that places named 'Caldecote' or 'Caldecot' etc. (i.e. 'the cold hut') are unusually often located in marginal positions, such as near a shire border, and argued that they denote places of banishment. Interestingly, the only such place in Oxfordshire (in its pre-1974 boundaries), now known as 'Caulcott', but first attested in 1199 as 'Caldecot', is just 500-700 m from Aves Ditch (**fig. 7**). This led Tallon (1999: 46 no. 34) to conclude (independently, whilst he and I were still unaware of having come at the same time, but on the basis of unrelated evidence, to similar conclusions) that 'Aves Ditch may once have formed a significant border here.' If Aves Ditch had indeed been created to mark a tribal boundary, as postulated above, and afterwards perhaps the extent of the Roman *civitas* succeeding it, then Tallon's conclusion that the earthwork may still have functioned as a boundary in the Anglo-Saxon period is highly significant. It was the collective memory of people living in the area and the way the monument impacted on local geography which could have ensured that the earthwork retained this function for centuries and, quite possibly, for over a millennium. Still today substantial sections of it function as a parish boundary (and our small trench 1 extended from Upper Heyford in the west to Middleton Stoney in the east). Interestingly, some 700 m from Aves Ditch's southern terminal we find a Hoarstone Spinney (east of the intersection between Aves Ditch and the Kirtlington to Upper Heyford Road (the Port Way) on **fig. 7**), i.e. a 'boundary stone copse' (Gelling 1953: 225; cf. Winchester 2000: 53), even though it no longer forms any administrative boundary here today. While the major collective efforts involved in its construction are unlikely to have been remembered in the Anglo-Saxon period (as indicated by the naming of the earthwork and its contemporary counterparts, notably the Grim's Ditches), Aves Ditch still influenced the way people experienced the landscape and to an extent, determined how they moved across it (cf. Bradley 2000: 158). This functional longevity was probably partially due to the sheer physical effort which would have been involved in removing such a dominant landscape feature and untillable field boundary and partially due to information passed on from generation to generation. The latter phenomenon should not be underestimated and could explain the remarkable longevity of some boundaries in Britain, such as why a Bronze Age pit alignment underlies the modern parish boundary between Ashton Keynes and Somerford Keynes (Denison 1999).

Clusters of burials in association with boundary features and other re-used Roman or pre-Roman monuments occurred in the Roman period (Pearce 1998). In Anglo-Saxon times, a wide range of prehistoric monuments, such as linear earthworks and, more frequently, barrows, were re-used for unusual inhumations (Reynolds 1998; Semple 1998; Williams 1997). Recent radiocarbon dating even revealed a seventh-century beheaded burial at Stonehenge (**fig. 37**), which is near a hundred boundary, the dissection of the fourth neck vertebra in this case probably indeed indicating execution or, at least decapitation prior to decomposition (Pitts 2002). Reynolds (2002: 188) argues persuasively that 'the exclusion of social deviants to the limits of territories' seems to have been the aim of burials at such marginal positions rather than to provide the boundary with dead guardians as has been argued in other cases (cf. Charles-Edwards 1976 with reference to a separate head burial). Furthermore, it is possible that there may have been a belief that it would have been more difficult for the dead to escape from such a no man's land to take revenge on the living (Esmonde Cleary 2000: 137-8), as has been plausibly argued for a fourteenth-century possible murder victim, disposed of in a bog in south-west Sweden at the meeting-point of four parishes and, for added safety, pinned to the ground with wooden stakes (Glob 1969: 148-51). Even if no attempt can be offered here to try to establish if and how the different traditions relate to each other, it is worth emphasising that the idea that boundary territory outside a community was the appropriate place to cast out the bodies of those guilty of major violations of its laws, whether for religious or profane reasons, appears to have been widespread in the ancient and medieval world (cf. Pl., *Leg.* 873b-874b).

The vicinity of traffic routes and crossroads was equally suitable for the execution (for reasons of ease of reach, visibility and deterrence) and later burial of wrongdoers (Reynolds 1998; 2002: 181-3) in the Anglo-Saxon period (and similar ideas occur much earlier [Pl., *Leg.* 873b; cf. Saunders 1991: 242 no. 136]). Aves Ditch almost certainly formed a traffic route at the time and it is likely that some of the current roads and rights of way have a long tradition.

Figure 37. Stonehenge, the most famous prehistoric monument to have yielded a decapitated Anglo-Saxon burial (between the outer circle and the ditch, roughly at the right edge of the photo), probably an execution victim, was a site dominating the landscape and located in the vicinity of a hundred boundary.

Figure 38. The crossroads south of the Gorse between the Middleton Stoney – Lower Heyford road, the public footpath along Aves Ditch and a footpath to Upper Heyford on 9 November 1997: trench 1 was c. 60 m from these crossroads in the woods on the right; the stone wall on the left marks the continuation of Aves Ditch to the south.

Currently, Aves Ditch and a second traffic route intersect just 60 m SSW of our trench 1, a third public footpath, leading to the north-west, branches off the latter near the same road junction. Old maps (e.g. Davis 1797) suggest that all these routes have a long tradition. It is thus likely that the burial lay even in the Anglo-Saxon period very close to crossroads (**figs 6, 15, 38**).

The mortal remains of the man buried in Aves Ditch provide no clue as to how he had died (see Hacking below). Since most causes of natural or violent death (e.g. hanging by strangulation) do not leave any traces on the skeleton, we cannot decide whether or not the Aves Ditch man had been formally executed or whether burial in consecrated ground had been denied to him for some other reason (e.g. suicide or dying guilty of a capital legal offence). Had he been the victim of a crime, then it seems unlikely that the perpetrator(s) would have chosen the vicinity of a traffic route, and probable crossroads, for his grave, where there would have been a higher risk of passers-by witnessing a clandestine burial. If we can thus conclude that he was probably not a victim of illegal homicide, it also seems unlikely that the removal of his head was motivated by a murderer's fear that the body might be exhumed and identified. Irrespective of the man's cause of death, the location of his last resting place suggests that he was a criminal in the eyes of his contemporaries, not worthy of a Christian burial.

In this context it would be interesting to know, whether this is an isolated burial or one of a number along Aves Ditch, and whether or not there is a distinct cluster near the crossroads; though even this would not necessarily allow us to decide whether or not we are dealing with an execution site, merely to assess whether or not we are dealing with a single event and single fate. Too little is known about the possibly Anglo-Saxon burials found in 1865 further north close to the Upper Heyford-Ardley parish boundary, widely thought to form the continuation of Aves Ditch. The association with 'stirrup irons and pieces of armour' (Meaney 1964: 209; Thurlow Leeds 1939: 372), however, argues against an interpretation as a burial site of execution victims or other social outcasts as far as this separate cemetery is concerned.

Yet, for people living in the area the story did not necessarily end with the burial of a criminal or social outcast. Ælfric attests in one of his homilies, when discussing a Biblical apparition, namely how the witch of Endor raised the prophet Samuel from the dead on the instigation of Saul (Samuel 1,28), that people in Anglo-Saxon England still believed in apparitions. Crossroad burials were sites where such evil ghostly apparitions occurred:

'Gyt farað wiccan to wega gelæton,
and to hæþenum byrgelsum mid heora gedwimore,
and clipiað to ðam deofle, and he cymð hym tó
on þæs mannes gelicnysse þe þær lið bebyrged,
swylce he of deaðe aríse; ...'

Witches still go to crossroads,
and to heathen burial places with their magical illusion,
and invoke the devil, and he comes to them
in the likeness of the person who lies buried there
as if the person were to rise from the dead ...

(Ælfric, Homilies, Supplementary Collection no. 29,118-22; edition: Pope 1968: 796; translation, based on Audrey Meaney as quoted by Reynolds 2002: 181 no. 38; Griffiths 1996: 35 and Bosworth and Toller 1898, cf. Meaney 1984-1985: 130-1, kindly checked, corrected and improved by Professor Don Scragg, who, however, is not responsible for any remaining shortcomings. See also Semple 1998: 113, 117.)

The homily is likely to date to the first decade of the eleventh century (information kindly supplied by Professor Scragg; cf. Pope 1967: 146-50, esp. 148), but there appears to be no certainty whether it pre- or postdates Ælfric's move from Cerne Abbas in Dorset to Eynsham in Oxfordshire in 1004/05 to become the abbot of a new monastery. Such clear and almost contemporary evidence for fear of the dead walking, associated with crossroad burials, renders it a high probability that the *post-mortem* beheading of the Aves Ditch man may be seen in such a context. Audrey Meaney (1984-1985: 130-1) stresses that crossroads and burials of evildoers or pagans, rather than Christian cemeteries, were deliberately chosen for such evil magic. Contemporary beliefs in the powers of darkness residing not only at crossroads and the places of non-consecrated human burials, but also at ancient boundary dykes and banks, add further strength to the theory that the interment of the man in Aves Ditch and the later mutilation of his bodily remains are likely to be related to such religious fears. Sarah Semple (1998: 115-16) has pointed out that prehistoric linear earthworks frequently formed boundaries and were often named after Grim (such as the Oxfordshire Grim's Ditches), i.e. probably the pagan Germanic god Wodan (cf. Simek 1984: 144, 466; Wilson 1992: 20-1). She makes a powerful case that the Anglo-Saxons from the eighth century onwards considered such boundaries and boundary dykes, like ancient burial mounds, to be 'evil and haunted places' and 'the haunt of monsters, spirits and evil creatures' (Semple 1998: 116, 123). The burial ground of the decapitated man at Aves Ditch was not only on such a dyke and boundary, but also next to, probably ancient, crossroads: undoubtedly, an ominous place in the eyes of his contemporaries, suitable for the burial of an outcast – yet not necessarily one where the dead would lie quiet. In this instance at least, we can go beyond David Wilson's (1992: 95, cf. 92-4) non-committal conclusions on the meaning of decapitation in Anglo-Saxon religion: 'From the limited evidence available, however, it seems likely that the practice would have been employed ... for ritual purposes whose real import and significance elude us.'

While nowhere near as close in terms of geography and cultural context as the passage in Ælfric, referring specifically to Anglo-Saxon England, it may, nevertheless, not be without interest to note that the Icelandic sagas provide unparalleled details on beliefs in north-west Europe at a broadly similar period (even if also slightly later) associated with ghostly apparitions and the countermeasures taken to combat them. Evil people buried in non-consecrated ground often did not lie quietly in their graves (*Eyrbyggja Saga*: 33-4, 63; *Grettir's Saga*: 32-5; *Laxdæla Saga*: 17, 24, 38; Keyser 1854: 304-7). Their burials were thus sometimes dug up long after their deaths and their remains reburied in remote regions (*Laxdæla Saga*: 17, 76; *Eyrbyggja Saga*: 34) or, since this did not necessarily prevent the restless dead from committing further misdeeds, burnt and the ashes buried far away from any habitations or scattered in the sea (*Grettir's Saga*: 35; *Laxdæla Saga*: 24; *Eyrbyggja Saga*: 63). Heads may have been considered particularly ominous (cf. *Eyrbyggja Saga*: 43), and *post-mortem* beheadings of the ghosts in heroic struggles are equally reported, the head then being placed next to the thighs or buttocks ('við þjó') of the corpse (*Grettir's Saga*: 18, 35); this could, but need not necessarily, be followed by cremation of the remains. These were the only effective ways to stop the ghosts from haunting the living and from killing domestic animals and human beings, who lived in, or ventured into, the reach of their nightly wanderings in the surroundings of their burial sites.

We also hear of a woman digging up the body of her slain husband (guilty of instigating attempted murder) and removing his head in order to use it as a powerful reminder to a reluctant kinsman that his killers should be brought to justice (*Eyrbyggja Saga*: 26-7). As the Aves Ditch corpse had largely decomposed by the time it was affected by the same sort of intervention and as it does not appear to have been a regular burial of a respected member of the community, it seems unlikely that it was dug up for similar reasons as the last-mentioned example, but the Icelandic parallel serves to demonstrate that such a violation of the sanctity of a grave on a private initiative was not necessarily as unthinkable in this period as it would be for us today.

It ought to be stressed, of course, that the Aves Ditch burial almost certainly predates any major Viking penetration into this part of Britain and that, despite some common heritage between the Anglo-Saxons and the ancestors of the settlers of Iceland, any assumption of a direct link would be highly speculative. Nevertheless, broadly similar traditions often have a much longer lifetime and manifest themselves in much wider territories than some experts in specific archaeological cultures, favouring an ahistorical approach, would have us believe (Karl 2004; Sauer 2004b: 14). The question ought not to be whether the possibility that Icelandic sagas could provide a possible model should be rejected as a matter of principle, but whether, if so, a more plausible explanation for the *post-mortem* beheading at Aves Ditch can be found. If not, then it seems fair to argue that the attested belief in apparitions in association with crossroad burials in Anglo-Saxon times could have inspired similar preventative action. Whether the same may already apply to some of the late Roman beheaded burials, is a question which goes beyond the scope of this study, but one would be inclined to see a difference between quite systematically severing the heads of a high proportion of corpses, predominantly shortly after death, in the late Roman period and the targeted action long after death at Aves Ditch in Anglo-Saxon times. This need not mean that those responsible for the intervention at Aves Ditch were not, consciously or unconsciously, influenced by the centuries-old local practice of *post-mortem* beheading, but, more probably, their action reflects a complex network of constantly evolving, interacting and partially merging ritual traditions and beliefs, of which the old local practice may have formed one strong, but not the sole root.

It is clear that those who exhumed the skull knew precisely where to dig. This need not be surprising, as the grave could easily have been marked in an archaeologically untraceable manner (e.g. by a pile of stones, removed subsequently) or, after a few years, ground disturbance could still have been visible or some minor subsidence could have revealed the location of the grave pit. I was involved a few years ago as a student helper in an excavation of an early medieval grave at Kirchheim am Neckar in south-west Germany where, in a similarly targeted intervention, though for quite different reasons, the belt region of a grave (where the most precious grave goods were normally kept) had been robbed and totally disturbed, while the remainder of the anatomy remained unaffected, equally without traces of surviving grave markings on the ground (Stork 1995: 233-4).

Whether the skull of the Aves Ditch man was buried, disposed of elsewhere or displayed is impossible to establish with certainty on the basis of the evidence presently available. The latter appears to have happened to a contemporary weathered skull, equally without lower jaw, of a c. 25-35 year-old woman who died between AD 647 and 877 (at 95.4% confidence) from Cottam (East Riding of Yorkshire) and is thought to be possibly an execution victim (Richards 2000: 36-7, 85-6, 92-4; Reynolds 1998: 9; 2002: 187). By contrast, the fragmentation *in situ* of the Aves Ditch skull, as indicated by the small fragment left behind, rather argues against display, and its reburial, casting away or destruction by fire or other means are more likely alternatives.

CONCLUSIONS: AVES DITCH, A PUZZLE SOLVED – OR A PERPETUAL ENIGMA?

It ought to be reiterated that there can be no 'guarantee' that the hypothesis that Aves Ditch was constructed to mark and protect the Catuvellaunian boundary is correct. Despite all the indications to the contrary, we cannot even disprove that it might have been a linear earthwork of a different function or exclude the possibility that it might have been a road after all. The clear orientation of Aves Ditch towards Tackley Ford and its straight alignment are still the strongest arguments for a road and the most puzzling aspects of its proposed interpretation as a linear earthwork, notwithstanding the observation that an orientation of an earthwork towards the ford in the Iron Age would be perfectly conceivable, for reasons stated above. Should future excavations find traces of O'Neil's (1929: 33) postulated link between the earthwork and Crowcastle Lane, then this case would be strengthened. Those, who would prefer to see it as a Roman road, will also point to the width of its *agger*, which, however, would by no means be unusual for an Iron Age earthwork. Should it indeed have been constructed as a Roman road, then the most likely context is the immediate post-conquest period, in the light of the absence of Roman artefacts from the *agger* or the bottom silt of the ditch and the fact that, if intended to be a road, it was abandoned after only a short stretch had been built. An ambitious road-building programme seems to have been initiated in the area shortly after the conquest. Two other roads in the area appear not to have been completed and both date to the mid-first century: the above mentioned road leading through the AD 44 gate at Alchester towards the ford at Tackley, but untraceable on aerial photographs beyond the line of the modern A41 (Sauer 2001: 2 fig. 1, 14; Booth *et al.* 2002: 3 fig. 1.2), and a road leading from Alchester to the south-east, sectioned twice in 1998. The latter has so far been traced archaeologically over a distance of 550 m, but a modern lane almost certainly follows it for about another 2 km (Sauer 1999a; 1999e: 290 fig. 6, 292 fig. 7, 295). Beyond this point no certain traces of it have ever been found. However, there are significant structural differences between these roads (both with copious Roman material from the road-side ditches, though this may be the result of the vicinity of Alchester) and Aves Ditch: unlike Aves Ditch, they both have road-side ditches on either side and the height differential between the bottom of the ditch and the preserved top of the paving never amounted to more than c. 1.10 m, even when they, unlike most of Aves Ditch, lead through terrain liable to flooding.

Furthermore, the difference to Sungbo's Eredo, a c. 160 km-long earthwork in Nigeria of c. AD 1000, may be worth noting. While the latter entirely encloses a territory of c. 30 x 40 km, and appears to be interrupted only where swamp forests made an artificial boundary impossible and unnecessary and has been reasonably interpreted as a boundary rampart of a local kingdom (Darling 1997; 1998: 9-11), the Oxfordshire linear earthworks do not enclose a tribal territory, but, if functioning as boundaries, merely skirt it on one side. The question thus arises whether this indicates that they did not function as political boundaries or that there was particular pressure or some other need in the far south-west of Catuvellaunian territory and/or whether the initiative to construct it came from a subgroup of the tribe.

There is thus no claim here that the possibility that the bank of Aves Ditch was a road or an earthwork of a different, though as yet unexplained, function, can be ruled out. Yet, the indications for its interpretation as a boundary marker are, in my view at least, stronger.

I. Several arguments suggest that it is unlikely to have functioned as a road:
I.1. No stream or wet ground can explain the, for a Roman road entirely unnecessary, monumentality of the southern part of Aves Ditch and many other sections in terrain not liable to flooding.
I.2. Its labour-intensive construction also elsewhere would not be typical for a road or minor earthwork. While there are substantial variations from section to section, the dimensions of the ditch of the North Oxfordshire Grim's Ditch and (where preserved) the width and height

of the bank are on average similar to those of Aves Ditch. In the light of the bow-shaped course of the North Oxfordshire Grim's Ditch, we can safely exclude that it was a road. It is thus at least perfectly possible that Aves Ditch, an, on the basis of the embedded artefacts, contemporary monument of similar dimensions, functioned as an earthwork as well.

I.3. That there was a ditch only on one side, rather than on both, would be unusual for a road, even if not entirely inconceivable (since the ditch was not just for drainage, but also the quarry for the *agger*).

I.4. Unless future evidence proves that O'Neil's (1929) above-cited tentatively identified rise in the ground between Aves Ditch's southern terminal and Crowcastle Lane was part of the monument, no *agger* was available to allow the traveller to continue his or her journey along the over 1 km-long gap between the ford and the monument's southern terminal, nor did a hollow way evolve. This suggests that not even a track followed this line, and certainly not one used intensively for a noteworthy period of time.

I.5. Aves Ditch starts and ends at points where there are no topographical or other obvious logical reasons for bringing a road, or the paved section of a road, to an end.

I.6. Perhaps most importantly: there is no obvious destination for the road. The strong indications for a very early, and barely post first-century, construction date, raises the question what would have motivated any authority or individual to make such a major investment of labour to link scarcely more than a few minor peasant settlements, at a time when much more important traffic infrastructure still had to be created.

II. It is unlikely to have been a Roman military construction, as most of the Roman military linear barriers are later than the date suggested for Aves Ditch on the basis of the associated artefact assemblage (or the date of the military occupation of Alchester, i.e. AD 43/44-AD 50s or early AD 60s [Sauer 2005], if thought to be associated with this nearby mid-first century fortress).

III. There are parallels for similar Iron Age installations and circumstantial evidence for its possible function as marking or protecting a tribal boundary.

III.1. It is worth emphasising that (in contrast to the above-cited West African example of Sungbo's Eredo) in none of the cases where there is written testimony for tribal boundaries being marked or defended by earthworks in the ancient world, is there anything to suggest that they ever surrounded the tribal territory in its entirety. If the Catuvellauni, or a subgroup of them, constructed such barriers just on one side, then this would have been the norm rather than the exception.

III.2. The, presumably contemporary, South and North Oxfordshire Grim's Ditches, neither of which is in an obvious location for a Roman military barrier, furthermore suggest that the late Iron Age population was capable of building linear earthworks similar to Aves Ditch.

III.3. The presence of late Iron Age material, and the absence of distinctive Roman artefacts from the bank and earliest ditch fill, renders a late Iron Age or invasion-period construction date likely. In the absence of an obvious parallel for a similar early post-conquest monument (cf. I and II), the interpretation as a late Iron Age earthwork gains in probability.

III.4. The location of both Aves Ditch and the South Oxfordshire Grim's Ditch, where other indications, notably numismatic evidence, suggest the boundary of the Catuvellauni was, is unlikely to be coincidental.

III.5. That the ditch is in both cases facing away from Catuvellaunian territory is a further piece of circumstantial evidence for associating these two barriers with this particular tribe.

III.6. That Aves Ditch appears to have retained a boundary function for centuries after its construction may suggest a long-term functional continuity. It ought to be conceded, however, that the observation that it may well have formed a boundary in the early Middle Ages (even if this was certain) does not on its own prove that it could not originally have been erected for a different purpose.

III.7. Written evidence leaves no doubt that linear barriers, some of which (notably the *agger* of the Angrivarii), according to their description, appear to have been similar to Aves Ditch, existed at least in parts of northern Europe. There is also archaeological evidence for similar earthworks in probable boundary zones (e.g. the Olgerdiget).

Aves Ditch has not given up all of its secrets and the debate will, no doubt, continue. Should in future further sections emerge which link it securely with Tackley ford and a sufficiently major Roman settlement in the north (though the latter in particular seems unlikely), then its interpretation as a Roman road would gain greater probability. However, while there is still no certainty why this mysterious monument was constructed some 2,000 years ago, on the basis of the evidence available at the present moment, its interpretation as a linear earthwork and, probably, tribal boundary marker, seems in my view the most plausible amongst the options on offer.

EPILOGUE

Notwithstanding the levelling of substantial parts, Aves Ditch with its over four kilometres long, and mostly tree-lined, straight section has remained one of the most intriguing, inspiring and thought-provoking ancient landmarks in Oxfordshire. The visitor to the remains in the Gorse in particular will be impressed by the substantial efforts which must have been involved in its construction. It is a landscape feature which had deep meaning for the local population throughout most of the first millennium and probably beyond. It is hoped that what is left of it will be enjoyed by many future generations and not obliterated by modern earth-moving operations, construction works or mechanised agriculture as have so many other ancient earthworks all over the world.

THE CONTEXTS

by Eberhard W. Sauer

Contexts were numbered during the 1997/98, but not during the 1937 excavations. Deposits are marked by context numbers, consisting of a number, or a number followed by a letter. It is appreciated that the latter is unconventional, but it is perfectly logical (even if potentially confusing) which is why these context labels were retained. Contexts marked with the same number, but a different letter were deposits thought to be just a single unit when first encountered, but later subdivided if they proved to consist of separate units of different composition and/or relative age. Thus they should now be regarded as separate deposits and not as subdivisions of one. For significant finds from the 1997/98 excavation not just the context, but also the three-dimensional position has been recorded. They have been plotted onto the profile of **fig. 16**, on the basis of their height above the sea-level and their position with regard to the long axis of trenches 1 to 2, but neglecting the third dimension, similar to the way the 1937 finds have been plotted onto the respective sections. In a few instances contexts have been totally renumbered, where it was felt that the original attribution of numbers was misleading. In case of renumbered or subdivided contexts, care has been taken to check that the associated finds were relabelled as well. In these instances the original context numbers (Sauer 1999d: 66 fig. 26) should now be disregarded. No experienced excavator will be surprised by the observation that the boundary between deposits was often diffuse and that the successive construction of the bank out of material from different locations, transported from the ditch to the bank, probably in small loads of soil and stones by individuals, did not always result in sharp and well-defined boundaries, and neither did the successive silting-up of the ditch over two millennia. The three-dimensional position of finds is thus at least as important for their interpretation as their secure or tentative attribution to a particular context. Cuts are not plotted on **fig. 16**, but their position should be clear on the basis of the description provided in the tabular list below.

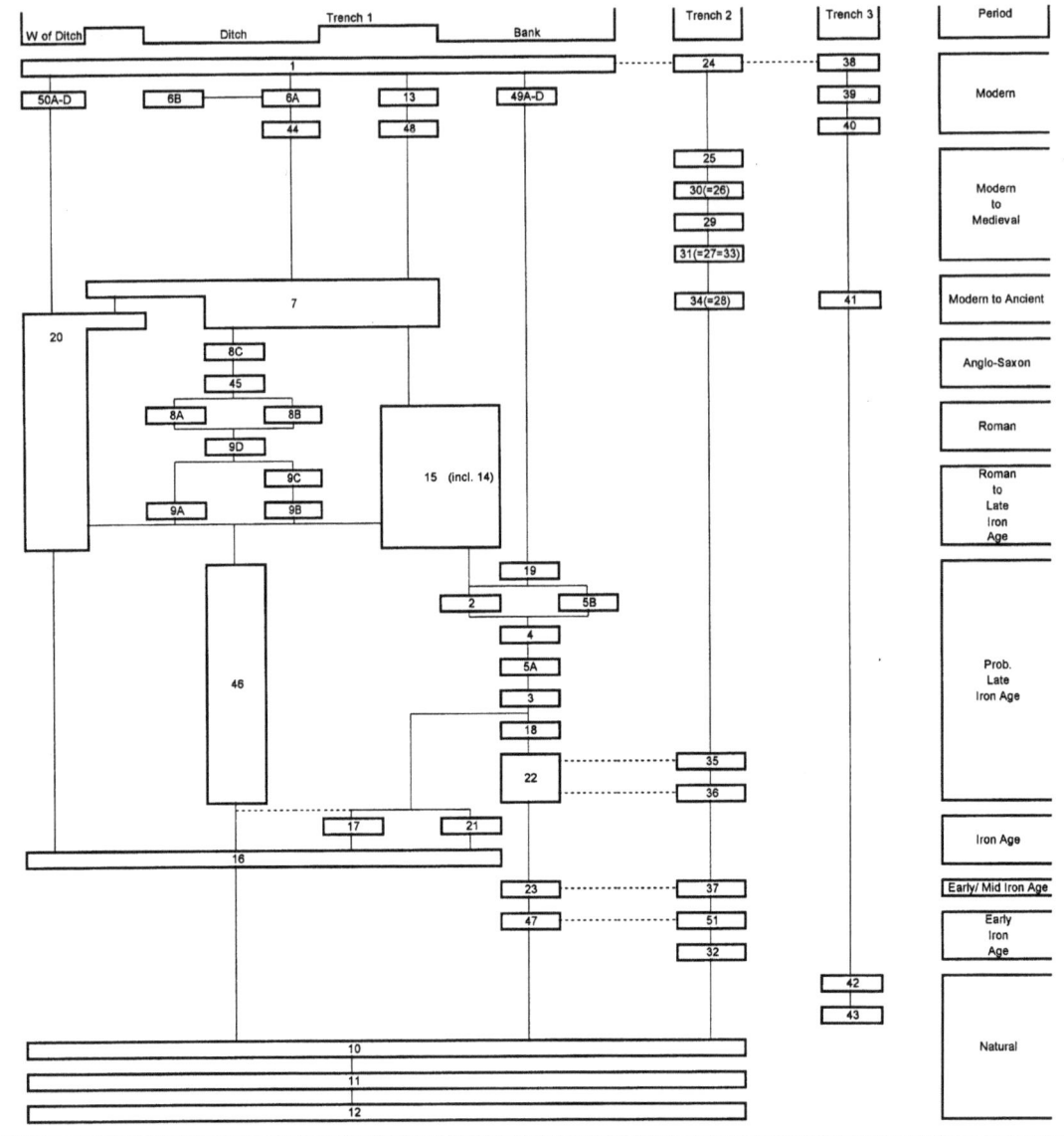

Figure 39. Stratigraphic matrix of trenches 1, 2 and 3.

Table 1: the contexts (cf. **fig. 39**)

Con-text	Trench	Type	Younger than	Contempo-rary with	Older than	Date/period	Soil	Stone inclu-sions (esti-mated)	Interpreta-tion	Comments	Fig.
1	1	De-posit	Overlies 6A & 13, fills 49a-d & 50a-d	Prob. 24 & 38	-	Modern	Soft dark-brown silt	c. 5%	Topsoil	n/a	**Fig. 16 a, b & c**
2	1	De-posit	Overlies 4	Abuts 5B	Overlain by 19; cut by 49A & B	Prob. late Iron Age/ c. 2nd ¼ 1st c. AD	Soft mid-yellow silt	c. 80%	Part of the stone bank of Aves Ditch	Material prob. quarried from bedrock/ bottom of ditch	**Fig. 16 b & c**
3	1	De-posit	Overlies 17, 18 & 21	-	Overlain by 5A	Prob. late Iron Age/ c. 2nd ¼ 1st c. AD	Soft mid-reddish brown clayey silt	c. 10-15%	Lower part of bank of Aves Ditch	Material prob. from ancient top and subsoil/ top of ditch	**Fig. 16 b & c**
4	1	De-posit	? Over-lies 5A	-	? Over-lain by 2 & 5B	Poss. late Iron Age/ c. 2nd ¼ 1st c. AD or later	Very soft mid-brown clayey silt	c. 3%	Decayed wood, tree root or animal burrow at the inter-face of the deposits with high and low stone con-tent, form-ing the bank	n/a	**Fig. 16 c**
5A	1	De-posit	Overlies 3	-	Overlain by 4	Prob. late Iron Age/ c. 2nd ¼ 1st c. AD	Soft mid-yellow silt	c. 5%	Middle part of bank of Aves Ditch	Material prob. from ancient subsoil/ middle layers of ditch	**Fig. 16 c**
5B	1	De-posit	Overlies 4	Abuts 2	Overlain by 19	Prob. late Iron Age/ c. 2nd ¼ 1st c. AD	Very soft light-yellowish brown silt	c. 15%	Middle part of bank of Aves Ditch	Material prob. from ancient subsoil/ middle layers of ditch	**Fig. 16 c**
6A	1	De-posit	Fill of 44	Abuts 6B	Overlain by 1	Modern	Firm dark-brown clayey silt	c. 1%	Fill of mod-ern ditch	Maybe for a modern hedge, poss. associated with the parish boundary; humus suggests washed-in rotted organic matter or topsoil, which may, but need not, be associ-ated with the possi-ble hedge; contained china and other modern finds	**Fig. 16 b**

Con-text	Trench	Type	Younger than	Contempo-rary with	Older than	Date/period	Soil	Stone inclu-sions (esti-mated)	Interpreta-tion	Comments	Fig.
6B	1	De-posit	See 6A	Abuts 6A	See 6A	Modern	Firm dark-brown clayey silt	c. 1%	Decayed root or animal borrow	See 6A; the inter-pretation of the protrusion as a root would offer poss. support for a modern hedge/ scrub	**Fig. 16 b**
7	1	De-posit	Overlies 8C, 15 & 20	-	Cut by 44 & 48	3rd/ 9th c. to modern	Very soft light-brown clayey silt	c. 1%	Upper fill of Aves Ditch	Prob. the result of the slow silting up of the ditch over more than a millen-nium, but with a prob. much increased rate of sediment accumula-tion in post-medieval times	**Fig. 16 a & b**
8A	1	De-posit	Overlies 9D	? 8B	Cut by 45	Prob. Roman	Very soft light-brown clayey silt	c. 3%	Fill of Aves Ditch, pre-dating grave cut	Low stone content may indicate that much of the material was washed/ deposited into the ditch from the west, i.e. away from the bank	**Fig. 16 b**
8B	1	De-posit	Overlies 9D	? 8A	Cut by 45	Prob. Roman	Very soft light-brown clayey silt	c. 20%	Fill of Aves Ditch, pre-dating grave cut	Higher stone concentra-tion probably derives from the bank	**Fig. 16 b**

Con-text	Trench	Type	Younger than	Contempo-rary with	Older than	Date/ period	Soil	Stone inclu-sions (esti-mated)	Interpreta-tion	Comments	Fig.
8C	1	De-posit	Fill of 45	-	Overlain by 7	Late 7th to 9th c. (see carbon-14 date for skele-ton above)	Very soft light-brown clayey silt	c. 20-80%	Fill of grave cut	Prob. re-deposited material from 8A, 8B & 9D resulting in irreg. stone concentra-tion; borders to 8A and 8B diffuse and mainly based on generally higher stone concentra-tion (prob. as a result of mixing stone-rich re-deposited material from 9D with less stony material from 8A and 8B)	**Fig. 16 b**
9A	1	De-posit	Bottom fill of 46, postdat-ing lower parts of 20	? 9B	Overlain by 9D	Prob. late Iron Age to early Roman	Very soft light-yellowish brown clayey silt	c. 5%	Primary fill of Aves Ditch	Low stone content indicates that much of the material was washed into the ditch from the west, i.e. away from the bank	**Fig. 16 b**
9B	1	De-posit	Bottom fill of 46, postdat-ing lower parts of 15	? 9A	Overlain by 9C	Prob. late Iron Age to early Roman	Friable light-brown clayey silt	c. 20%	Primary fill of Aves Ditch	Higher stone concentra-tion probably derives from early natural erosion of the bank	**Fig. 16 b**

Con-text	Trench	Type	Younger than	Contempo-rary with	Older than	Date/period	Soil	Stone inclu-sions (esti-mated)	Interpreta-tion	Comments	Fig.
9C	1	De-posit	Overlies 9B	-	Overlain by 9D	Prob. late Iron Age to early Roman	Friable light-brown clayey silt	c. 20%	Secondary-phase fill of Aves Ditch	Higher stone concentra-tion probably derives from natural erosion of the bank, but much lower stone concentra-tion than in 9D suggests that it, 9A and 9B predate the postulated levelling of the bank	**Fig. 16 b**
9D	1	De-posit	Overlies 9A & 9C	-	Overlain by 8A & 8B (cut by 45)	Prob. early Roman	Very soft light-brown clayey silt	c. 80%	Material from the bank re-deposited into Aves Ditch	Result of erosion of the bank and, prob., of inten-tional re-deposition to trans-form the bank into a track	**Fig. 16 b**
10	1	Natu-ral deposit	Overlies 11	-	Overlain by 16 and 32, cut by 47 (, 46 & 51)	Natural	Friable mid-brownish yellow silt	c. 95%	Natural bedrock	n/a	**Fig. 16 a & b**
11	1	Natu-ral deposit	Overlies 12	-	Overlain by 10 (cut by 46)	Natural	Friable mid-yellow silt	c. 0%	Natural deposit	n/a	**Fig. 16 b**
12	1	Natu-ral deposit	-	-	Overlain by 11 (cut by 46)	Natural	-	c. 100%	Solid lime-stone bed-rock	n/a	**Fig. 16 b**
13	1	De-posit	Fill of 48	? Might be roughly contempo-rary with 6A	Overlain by 1	Prob. modern	Soft dark-brown clayey silt	c. 50%	Deposit with oblique to vertical layering of stones, which ap-peared to fill a hole	Fill of pulled-out recent post (perhaps of 19th-c. fence [cf. Anon. 1842: 6]?) or scrub or tree root?	**Fig. 16 b**
14	See 15	See 15	See 15	Part of 15	See 15	See 15	See 15	See 15	See 15	Originally treated as a possible posthole, but evi-dence (i.e. layering of stones) insuffi-cient; cf. 15	**Fig. 16 b**

Con-text	Trench	Type	Younger than	Contempo-rary with	Older than	Date/period	Soil	Stone inclu-sions (esti-mated)	Interpreta-tion	Comments	Fig.
15	1	De-posit	Overlies 2	See 14	Overlain by 7; the lower parts of this deposit must be earlier than 9B	Lower parts prob. late Iron Age to early Roman; upper parts prob. later Roman	Soil varies from very soft mid-brown clayey silt to very soft mid-brownish yellow silt	c. 40% (on average, but with consid-erable varia-tions)	Deposit with obliquely layered stones as a result of the erosion of the bank	Deposit is likely to have built up succes-sively, as a result of erosion, over several centuries; cf. 14	**Fig. 16 b**
16	1	De-posit	Overlies 10	-	Overlain by 20; predat-ing 17 & 21; cut by 46 (similar deposit prob. also cut by 47, but 16 may well have been culti-vated later)	Iron Age	Soft mid-brownish yellow silt	c. 10%	Iron Age topsoil	Cf. 17	**Fig. 16 a & b**
17	1	De-posit	Later than 16	Prob. 21	Overlain by 3, prob. earlier than 46	Iron Age	Irregular vertical bands of very soft mid-brown clayey silt	c. 0%	Prob. Iron Age scrub or tree roots	Originally treated as a possible posthole, but evi-dence insuffi-cient; cf. 16	**Fig. 16 b**
18	1	De-posit	Overlies 22	-	Overlain by 3	Prob. late Iron Age/ c. 2nd ¼ 1st c. AD	Soft mid-reddish brown clayey silt	c. 5%	Prob. deliberately deposited to complete levelling the ground over the curving ditch and to form the lowest part of the bank of Aves Ditch	Low percentage of stone inclusions indicates that prob. re-deposited ancient topsoil; the curv-ing ditch still seems to have formed a shallow depression in the area of trench 1, when the bank of Aves Ditch was con-structed, even after its rock-cut section had been filled up with stony material (see 22).	**Fig. 16 b & c**

Con-text	Trench	Type	Younger than	Contempo-rary with	Older than	Date/period	Soil	Stone inclu-sions (esti-mated)	Interpreta-tion	Comments	Fig.
19	1	De-posit	Overlies 2 & 5B	-	Cut by 49C & D	Prob. late Iron Age/ c. 2nd ¼ 1st c. AD	Gradual transition, from top to bot-tom, from very soft dark-brown to soft mid-brown clayey silt	c. 75%	Top of bank of Aves Ditch	Material prob. quarried from bedrock/ bottom of ditch; bioturba-tion and/or plant roots are likely to account for darker colour of top.	**Fig. 16 c**
20	1	De-posit	Overlies 16	-	Cut by 50A, B, C & D, overlain by 7; lower parts predate 9A	Late Iron Age or early Roman to Roman, medie-val or early modern	Very soft light-brown clayey silt	c. 25%	Old topsoil	Includes material washed down the slope towards the ditch.	**Fig. 16 a**
21	1	De-posit	Later than 16	Prob. 17	Overlain by 3, prob. earlier than 46	Iron Age	Friable mid-yellowish brown silt	c. 50%	Small depression, filled with darker material than sur-rounding area, of uncertain, but no structural significance	Round discolour-ation of 0.35 m diam. with a shallow and irreg. profile, 9.75-10.10 m E, 0-0.35 m S of profile line	Not plotted
22	1	De-posit	Overlies 23	Prob. 35 & 36	Overlain by 18	Prob. late Iron Age/ c. 2nd ¼ 1st c. AD	Very soft mid-brown clayey silt	c. 50%	Upper fill of curving ditch	The high percentage of stone inclusions suggests that this section of the curv-ing ditch was delib-erately filled in, rather than being allowed to silt up naturally, prob. immedi-ately prior to the construc-tion of the bank; the high stone content may have been deliberate to reduce the risk of later subsi-dence.	**Fig. 16 b & c**

Con-text	Trench	Type	Younger than	Contempo-rary with	Older than	Date/period	Soil	Stone inclu-sions (esti-mated)	Interpreta-tion	Comments	Fig.
23	1	De-posit	Bottom fill of 47	Prob. 37	Overlain by 22	c. 500-325 BC, prob. 500-410 BC (bot-tom); upper parts may repre-sent slow silting-up of ditch in the mid to late Iron Age	Soil varies from very soft light-reddish brown and very soft light-yellowish brown to very soft mid-brown clayey silt	Varies from c. 2% at the sides to c. 15% in the centre	Bottom fill of curving ditch	Low stone content and the observa-tion that the archaeo-magnetic samples were datable (i.e. probably water-borne sediments) suggest that this deposit represents natural silting up of the ditch. The lower percentage of stone inclusions at the sides is prob. the result of fine mate-rial being washed in at an early date.	**Fig. 16 b & c**
24	2	De-posit	Overlies 25	Prob. 1 & 38	-	Modern	Soft dark-brown silt	c. 5%	Topsoil	n/a	**Fig. 16 c**
25	2	De-posit	Overlies 30	-	Overlain by 24	Medie-val/ modern	Very soft mid-reddish brown clayey silt	c. 4%	Medieval/ earlier modern layer	Low stone content indicates that mate-rial does not derive from the stone bank, but prob. from the E.	**Fig. 16 c**
26	See 30	See 30	See 30	See 30	See 30	See 30	See 30	See 30	See 30	Same as 30	See 30
27	See 31	See 31	See 31	See 31	See 31	See 31	See 31	See 31	See 31	Same as 31	See 31
28	See 34	See 34	See 34	See 34	See 34	See 34	See 34	See 34	See 34	Same as 34	See 34
29	2	De-posit	Overlies 31	-	Overlain by 30	Medie-val/ modern	Very soft mid-brown clayey silt	c. 80%	Eroded/ re-deposited material from the stone bank	Extending only 0.04 m (on S-facing profile) to 0.28 m (on N-facing profile) into trench 2, but clearly visible as a distinct 0.04 to 0.20 m thick band sloping into the ditch on the E-facing profile.	**Fig. 16 c**

Con-text	Trench	Type	Younger than	Contempo-rary with	Older than	Date/ period	Soil	Stone inclu-sions (esti-mated)	Interpreta-tion	Comments	Fig.
30	2	De-posit	Overlies 29	-	Overlain by 25	Medie-val/ modern	Very soft mid-brown to mid-reddish brown clayey silt	c. 5-8%	Medieval/ earlier modern layer	Low stone content indicates that mate-rial does not derive from the stone bank, but prob. from the E.; cf. 26	**Fig. 16 c**
31	2	De-posit	Overlies 34	-	Overlain by 29	Medie-val/ modern	Very soft mid-yellowish to light-reddish brown clayey silt	From c. 10-20 % stone inclu-sions in the E to c. 50% in the W.	Medieval/ earlier modern layer	Higher stone concentra-tion in the west may be the result of the ero-sion of the stone bank; cf. 27 & 33.	**Fig. 16 c**
32	2	De-posit	Overlies 10	-	Cut by 51	Early Iron Age (prob. *termi-nus ante quem* = 500/ 410 BC [if 51 = 47])	Very soft yellow clayey silt	c. 2%	Unculti-vated(?) early Iron-Age topsoil	Similar absolute level as 16, but colour indicates no/ lower humus contents	**Fig. 16 c**
33	See 31	See 31	See 31	See 31	See 31	See 31	See 31	See 31	See 31	Same as 31	See 31
34	2	De-posit	Overlies 35	-	Overlain by 31	Roman, medie-val or modern	Very soft light-yellowish to light-greyish brown silt	c. 20%	Uppermost fill of curving ditch	n/a	Not shown
35	2	De-posit	Overlies 36	Prob. 22	Overlain by 34	Prob. late Iron Age/ c. 2nd ¼ 1st c. AD	Very soft dark greyish-brown clayey silt	c. 80%	Upper fill of curving ditch	High stone content suggests that also this sec-tion of the curving ditch was deliber-ately filled in, even if the bank did not extend to trench 2: maybe for ease of movement along the E/ inside of the earthwork	Not shown
36	2	De-posit	Overlies 37	Prob. 22	Overlain by 35	Prob. late Iron Age/ c. 2nd ¼ 1st c. AD	Very soft light-yellowish brown clayey silt	c. 80%	Lower fill of curving ditch	See 35; probably earlier phase in deliberate filling-in of the curving ditch	Not shown

Con-text	Trench	Type	Younger than	Contempo-rary with	Older than	Date/period	Soil	Stone inclu-sions (esti-mated)	Interpreta-tion	Comments	Fig.
37	2	De-posit	Bottom fill of 51	Prob. 23	Overlain by 36	See 23: c. 500-325 BC, prob. 500-410 BC (bot-tom); upper parts may repre-sent slow silting-up of ditch in the mid to late Iron Age	Very soft light-yellowish brown clayey silt	From c. 5% at top to c. 1% at bottom	Bottom fill of curving ditch	Low stone content suggests that this deposit represents natural silting up of the ditch.	Not shown
38	3	De-posit	Overlies 39	Prob. 1 & 24	-	Modern	Soft dark-brown silt	c. 1%	Topsoil	n/a	Not shown
39	3	De-posit	Overlies 40	-	Overlain by 38	Modern	Soft dark-brown silt	c. 35%	Top of parish boundary bank	0.05 m-thick layer of stones to stabilise c. 0.40 m high bank	Not shown
40	3	De-posit	Overlies 41	-	Overlain by 39	Modern	Soft dark-brown silt	c. 1%	Bottom of parish boundary bank	Maybe built of material from 41	Not shown
41	3	De-posit	Overlies 42	-	Overlain by 40	Prehis-toric - modern	Soft mid-reddish brown clayey silt	c. 1%	Subsoil	Low percentage of stone inclusions provides a further argument against the stone bank of Aves Ditch ever having been extended to the immediate vicinity of trench 3	Not shown
42	3	De-posit	Overlies 43	-	Overlain by 41	Natural	Soft mid-reddish brown clayey silt	c. 80%	Natural deposit	Decayed plant roots and bio-turbation may account for colour difference to 43	Not shown
43	3	De-posit	-	-	Overlain by 42	Natural	Soft mid-yellow silt	c. 80%	Natural deposit	Cf. 42	Not shown
44	1	Cut	Cuts 7	Poss. 48?	Filled by 6A	Modern	-	-	Parish boundary ditch?	n/a	**See fig. 16 (cut not num-bered; see fill)**

Con-text	Trench	Type	Younger than	Contempo-rary with	Older than	Date/period	Soil	Stone inclu-sions (esti-mated)	Interpreta-tion	Comments	Fig.
45	1	Cut	Cuts 8A & 8B (& 9D)	-	Filled by 8C	Late 7th to 9th c. (see carbon-14 date for skele-ton above)	-	-	Grave cut	Cut almost impossible to see (as fill ap-pears to consist of same material as it was cut into) and precise line hypo-thetical	**See fig. 16 (cut not num-bered; see fill)**
46	1	Cut	Cuts (from top to bottom:) 16 (, 10, 11 & 12)	Bank and prob. artificial levelling of curving ditch (from bottom to top:) 22(?), 36(?), 35(?), 18, 3, 5A, 4, 2, 5B & 19	Filled by (from bottom to top:) 9A & 9B (& 9C, 9D, 8A, 8B, 8C, 7, 6A & 6B)	Prob. late Iron Age/ c. 2nd ¼ 1st c. AD	-	-	Ditch of Aves Ditch	The flat bottom of the cut is formed by a very hard layer of lime-stone bedrock	**See fig. 16 (cut not num-bered; see fill)**
47	1	Cut	Cuts 10 (may also have cut deposit similar to 16, but 16 may have been culti-vated later)	51	Filled by (from bottom to top): 23 (, 22 18 & parts of 3)	Prob. *termi-nus ante quem* = 500/ 410 BC	-	-	Curving ditch, prob. ditch around, or associated with, Iron-Age enclo-sure	47 and 51 are almost certainly part of the same cut	**See fig. 16 (cut not num-bered; see fill)**
48	1	Cut?	Later than (cuts?) 7	Poss. 44?	Older than (filled by?) 13	Modern	-	-	Recent post or scrub or tree root?	Cf. 13	**See fig. 16 (cut not num-bered; see fill)**
49A	1	Cut	Cuts 2, i.e. later than 19	49C	Filled by 1	Modern	-	-	Wheel rut	From 11.68-11.73 m E at the N profile to 11.59-11.76 m E at S pro-file	Not shown
49B	1	Cut	Cuts 2, i.e. later than 19	49D	Filled by 1	Modern	-	-	Wheel rut	From 12.15-12.20 m E, 0.44 m S of N profile to 12.00-12.13 m E at S pro-file	Not shown
49C	1	Cut	Cuts 19	49A	Filled by 1	Modern	-	-	Wheel rut	From 13.21-13.26 m E at the N profile to 13.18-13.26 m E at S pro-file	Not shown

Con-text	Trench	Type	Younger than	Contempo-rary with	Older than	Date/ period	Soil	Stone inclu-sions (esti-mated)	Interpreta-tion	Comments	Fig.
49D	1	Cut	Cuts 19	49B	Filled by 1	Modern	-	-	Wheel rut	From 13.70-13.74 m E at the N profile to 13.60-13.68 m E at S pro-file	Not shown
50A	1	Cut	Cuts 20	50C	Filled by 1	Modern	-	-	Wheel rut	From 0.80-0.96 m E at the N profile to 0.74-1.00 m E at S pro-file	Not shown
50B	1	Cut	Cuts 20	50D?	Filled by 1	Modern	-	-	Wheel rut	From 1.60-1.76 m E at the N profile to 1.66-1.90 m E at S pro-file; evi-dence slight; if paired with 50D unusually wide wheelbase	Not shown
50C	1	Cut	Cuts 20	50A (& D?)	Filled by 1	Modern	-	-	Wheel rut	From 2.31-2.47 m E at the N profile to 2.31-2.52 m E at S pro-file	Not shown
50D	1	Cut	Cuts 20	50B or C?	Filled by 1	Modern	-	-	Wheel rut	From 3.78-3.97 m E at the N profile to 3.81-4.05 m E at S pro-file	Not shown
51	2	Cut	Cuts (from top to bottom:) 32 (& 10)	47	Filled by (from bottom to top): 37 (, 36, 35, 34 & parts of 31)	Prob. *termi-nus ante quem* = 500/ 410 BC [if 51 = 47]	-	-	Curving ditch, prob. ditch around, or associated with, Iron-Age enclo-sure	47 and 51 are almost certainly part of the same cut	**See fig. 16 (cut not num-bered; see fill)**

73

THE POTTERY

by Paul Booth

Introduction

The excavations in 1937 and 1997-8 produced a small quantity of pottery – in total some 126 sherds weighing 635 grammes. The majority of the assemblage was of Iron Age date, with a smaller Roman component and occasional later pieces. The pottery was characteristically in quite poor condition, the sherds being typically quite abraded and having a very low mean sherd weight of just over 5 g. There were, however, differences between the material from the 1937 and the 1997-8 excavations, the latter generally producing larger sherds than the former. The mean weight of 3.5 g (2.9 g if the post-Roman sherds are excluded) and abraded condition of the sherds from the 1937 excavation made identification and dating especially difficult and the conclusions drawn from this material, in particular, must be treated with caution. Owing to the small sherd size it was usually difficult to determine if vessels were hand made or wheel thrown, thus rendering more problematic the task of distinguishing between pottery of middle Iron Age and late Iron Age (often wheel thrown) date, since these frequently share other characteristics such as fabric.

The pottery was recorded using the Oxford Archaeology's Iron Age and Roman pottery recording system, which by applying standardised codes for fabrics and forms allows easy comparison between assemblages from different parts of the region. Aspects of this are amplified below. Quantification was by sherd count, weight and a count of vessels based on individual rim sherds. Details of rim forms and other characteristics were recorded as appropriate but these were mostly completely absent.

Iron Age

One hundred sherds (459 g) were assigned to the early/middle Iron Age. The typical sherd size meant that fabric was usually the only diagnostic characteristic that could be recorded. Initial sorting of fabrics was done by eye, with subsequent use of a binocular microscope at x20 magnification to assist identification/ define the inclusion types of individual sherds. Only fairly summary fabric descriptions are given here.

Fabrics were generally defined in terms of their two most common inclusion types (see further below) and an indicator of fineness, on a scale from 1 (very fine) to 5 (very coarse), most fabrics falling in the middle of this range. The definition of fabrics using this system does not necessarily serve to identify production sources, since these are unknown for Iron Age material within the region. Nor does it automatically follow that identically-coded sherds were from the same (unknown) source, merely that their makers exploited very similar clay and tempering resources, indicating a uniformity of potting tradition. The range of inclusion types utilised was fairly broad, but most if not all would have been widely available or have occurred naturally in common clay sources in the region. No fabrics originating outside the Upper Thames region were identified. The range of inclusion types present, and their identifying letters, were as follows:

A   Quartz sand
C   Calcareous sand/ grit
G   Grog
I   Oxide minerals, mainly Iron oxides
L   Limestone
N   None visible
P   Clay Pellets

S Shell (includes 'modern' and fossil shell)
V Vegetable/ organic (sometimes voids)
Z Indeterminate voids

A substantial number of fabrics contained more than two inclusion types, but it was only rarely felt that these were particularly significant in terms of characterisation of the fabric, in which cases additional inclusion types were noted in recording. For the purposes of this report, however, such sherds have generally been grouped together in terms of their two principal inclusion types. Quantities of Iron Age and later pottery fabrics are listed by excavation trench in Table 2.

Table 2: Aves Ditch pottery fabric quantities (number of sherds and weight in grammes) by trench

Fabric/ware	1997-8				1937						TOTAL	
	Trench 1		Trench 2		Trench I		Trench II		Trench III and misc*			
	Nosh	Wt	Nosh	Wt	Nosh	Wt	Nosh	Wt	Nosh	Wt	Nosh	Wt
Iron Age												
ACV3			1	1							1	1
AG3			2	25					1	2	3	27
AL3			1	4							1	4
AS3	1	6					3	4			4	10
AV3	11	81	4	19	1	1					16	101
AZV3/4	2	6									2	6
CA3	1	1	1	4							2	5
CN3/4			7	20							7	20
CS3/4 & CSA3	5	48	1	10							6	58
CV3/4 & CVS3	17	100	4	9							21	109
CZ3	1	6	2	10							3	16
GAS3					1	1					1	1
LA4	1	4									1	4
LS4 & LSA4			3	15							3	15
LZ4			1	6							1	6
PAV3							1	1			1	1
S					3	<1					3	1
SA3/4					7	11	6	9			13	20
SA5			1	3							1	3
SG3					1	2	1	1	1*	<1*	3	4
SL4	1	28									1	28
SN4	1	12									1	12
SPA3					1	1					1	1
SV4	1	4			2	1					3	5
SZA3					1	1					1	1
Subtotal	*42*	*296*	*28*	*126*	*17*	*19*	*11*	*15*	*2*	*3*	*100*	*459*
Late Iron Age/Roman												
S30									1	<1	1	1
F25							1	3			1	3
F51									1	8	1	8
M22							1	15			1	15
W20	1	6									1	6
E20							1	5			1	5
E30					1	5					1	5
E40							1	1			1	1
E80	1	10					3	3			4	13
O10									1*	1*	1	1
O30					1	3					1	3
R10							1	3	5	43	6	46
R30							1	3			1	3
R37	1	12					1	8	1	7	3	27
C10	1	4									1	4
Subtotal	*4*	*32*	*-*	*-*	*2*	*8*	*10*	*41*	*9*	*60*	*25*	*141*
Medieval/post-medieval												
Z30									1	35	1	35
Subtotal									*1*	*35*	*1*	*35*
TOTAL	46	328	28	126	19	27	21	56	12	98	126	635

The assemblage consisted largely of sherds in three main tempering traditions: sand, calcareous grit and shell, comprising 27%, 39% and 28% respectively of the Iron Age sherd total. Minor fabric groupings with principal inclusion types of grog, clay pellets and limestone were also present. The distinction between some of these groupings was not always clear, particularly since, as already indicated, some sherds were so small that it was difficult to assess the true character of their inclusions precisely. There may therefore have been little meaningful difference between, for example, sherds tempered with limestone and sherds tempered with fossil shell which could have been derived from limestone. Generally, however, the three main traditions were considered to be distinct. Both sand and calcareous grit traditions are characteristic of the middle Iron Age in the region, and there may be an indication of their broad contemporaneity in the fact that organic (V) inclusions, plus voids (Z) that might have resulted from the complete burning-out of such inclusions, were the most common secondary tempering agents in both traditions in this assemblage. In contrast, shell-tempering is most important in the early Iron Age in the Upper Thames Valley. In the northern part of Oxfordshire, however, it is likely that shell-tempered traditions were maintained through the middle Iron Age (Booth 1998: 107). This situation could have prevailed here.

There were no decorated pieces and only four rim sherds in the whole group. From the 1998 excavation came a simple, tapered, slightly outsloping rim in fabric CV3 from trench 1 context 23, a very similar rim in fabric AL3 in trench 2 context 35/36 (both 4 g) and a larger, thickened upright sherd in fabric LS4 unstratified in trench 2. The only rim sherd from the 1937 excavation was a tiny fragment in fabric SA3 from trench I. None of these sherds was chronologically diagnostic. All would be consistent with a middle Iron Age date range, but an earlier date is also possible on purely typological grounds. For example, small fragments of rims from early Iron Age vessels such as the group from Kirtlington (Benson and Harding 1968) would not be significantly different from those of middle Iron Age vessel types.

In view of these typological characteristics, discussion of the chronology of the Iron Age assemblage has to be based entirely on the evidence of fabrics. The combined dominance of the sand and calcareous grit fabrics strongly suggests a middle Iron Age emphasis for the group. The shell-tempered fabrics could have been contemporary with this or they may indicate an earlier (i.e. early Iron Age) component in the assemblage. These issues are discussed further below.

Late Iron Age to Roman

Some 25 sherds (141 g) of pottery of this date were identified. The fabrics were placed in a number of major ware groups, defined on the basis of significant common characteristics and then subdivided hierarchically, as defined e.g. in Booth 1994: 135-6. The ware groups present were samian ware (S), fine wares - colour-coated, lead glazed, mica coated etc - (F), mortaria (M) and white wares - other than mortaria - (W) plus coarse ware groups: 'Belgic type'(in the sense of Thompson 1982: 4-5), usually grog-tempered, fabrics (E), 'Romanised' oxidised coarse wares (O) and 'Romanised' reduced coarse wares.

Within these classes the following specific fabrics or fabric subgroups were present:

S30   Central Gaulish samian ware
F25   Fine oxidised lead-glazed fabric
F51   Oxford red-brown colour-coated ware
M22   Oxford white *mortarium* fabric
W20   Sandy white ware fabrics
E20   Fine sand-tempered 'Belgic type' fabrics
E30   Coarse sand-tempered 'Belgic type' fabrics
E30   Shell-tempered 'Belgic type' fabrics

E80	Grog-tempered 'Belgic type' fabrics
O10	Fine oxidised 'coarse' wares, mostly Oxford products
O30	Fine sandy oxidised coarse wares
R10	Fine reduced 'coarse' wares, mostly Oxford products
R30	Moderately sandy reduced coarse wares
R37	Fine sandy reduced coarse ware
C10	Undifferentiated shell-tempered wares

The range of fabrics is generally unremarkable. A single tiny fragment of ?Central Gaulish samian ware was the only piece from a source outside the region. The other Romanised fabrics were mostly products of the Oxford industry, the only exception being fabric R37, for which a source in west Oxfordshire is likely (cf. Booth 1997a: 117). The most unusual item was a single sherd of a fine oxidised lead-glazed fabric (F25). This is tentatively attributed to the Oxford industry production site at Lower Farm, Nuneham Courtenay, where such fabrics were probably produced in the early second century AD (Booth *et al.* 1994: 137). A moderate component of 'Belgic type' wares, potentially of significance, was present, mainly in the 1937 trenches, and it is possible that the sherds assigned to fabrics GAS3 and SG3 in these trenches were also of this date, but they could not be assigned to the 'Belgic' tradition with confidence because of their size. These fabrics are widespread across the region and a local source is again likely.

Only two vessels, both undiagnostic jars or bowls, were represented by rim sherds, a tiny fragment in E80 from 1937 trench II and another in fabric R37 from context 8C in 1997 trench 1.

Overall the material spans the period from the early to mid-first century AD (the 'Belgic type' fabrics) to at least the mid to late third century. The sherds from 1997 trench 1, all from components of context 8, were probably all of first to second-century date, and as a group could even date entirely to the mid to late first century. The material from the 1937 trenches appears less coherent, but the single sherd of Oxford colour-coated ware (F51) from trench III, is the only piece that need necessarily have been of mid-third century or later date. The relative concentration of Roman material in this area may indicate Roman settlement in the vicinity.

Post-Roman

A single sherd of post-medieval date was present in the 1937 assemblage. This was a relatively superficial find in trench III. Fragments of ceramic building material of post-medieval date were also present in trenches I and III.

General Discussion

Recent work has added significantly to our understanding of the Iron Age ceramics of the area, with published assemblages from Steeple Aston (Brown 2001), Slade Farm, Bicester (Woodward and Marley 2001), Bicester Fields Farm (Brown 2000) and Alchester (Evans and Booth 2002), none more than 8 km distant from Aves Ditch, the first to the west and the others to the east.

Amongst these sites early Iron Age pottery was only present in modest quantities at Steeple Aston and Slade Farm, and the classic early Iron Age assemblage from the area remains that from Kirtlington (Benson and Harding 1968). Shell-tempering was characteristic of the early Iron Age material at Steeple Aston and Slade Farm, but at the latter site both coarse and fine calcareous-tempered fabrics were also associated with early Iron Age forms. Both shell and calcareous tempering traditions continued to be strongly represented there in the middle Iron

Age (Woodward and Marley 2001: 233), while at nearby Alchester the middle Iron Age assemblage was dominated by sherds with mixed calcareous temper (Evans and Booth 2002: 272). The middle Iron Age vessel forms are typically simple barrel or slightly globular shaped jars and bowls with few really distinctive characteristics and no decoration, except occasionally on globular bowl forms such as one from Slade Farm (Woodward and Marley 2001: 240 no. 14).

These traditions were eventually largely supplanted by the introduction of characteristic grog-tempered fabrics in the late Iron Age, although these fabrics could include other tempering agents as well, such as shell at Slade Farm. The most important assemblage of this period in the area is that from the settlement enclosure at Bicester Fields Farm. This site produced a moderately sized middle Iron Age assemblage and a rather larger late Iron Age one. It was also distinguished by having no significant early Roman activity - the only Roman features present related to a field system that was unassociated with contemporary settlement. While a similar cut-off in settlement sequence is likely to have occurred at Slade Farm, the dominant component of the pottery assemblage there seems to have been of middle Iron Age date, while at Alchester the assemblage was exclusively of that date, with no late Iron Age component at all. In contrast, a site at Oxford Road, Bicester produced a small quantity of middle Iron Age pottery and a more substantial late Iron Age assemblage but, unlike Slade Farm and Bicester Fields Farm, then saw continuous activity into the early Roman period (Booth 1997b), a sequence of development more characteristic of the Upper Thames valley as a whole (cf. Henig and Booth 2000: 106-7).

The middle Iron Age assemblage at Bicester Fields Farm, which may have been confined to the later part of that period (Brown 2000: 193), consisted essentially of sherds in the three main tempering traditions identified at Aves Ditch, though shell-tempered sherds slightly outnumbered the combined sand- and calcareous-tempered fabrics. The following late Iron Age assemblage contained a much smaller proportion of shell-tempered sherds in 'Belgic type' fabrics (only 6.6%) while sand-tempered fabrics were three time as common and the remainder (the bulk) of the assemblage was formed of grog-tempered sherds. It is notable that a large part of the late Iron Age assemblage at Bicester Fields Farm was handmade (*ibid.* 184), while at Slade Farm almost 60% of this material was recorded as wheelmade (Woodward and Marley 2001: 233). The significance of this difference is uncertain, but it is unlikely to be chronological as the two assemblages must have been closely contemporary. The condition of the Aves Ditch pottery precludes any attempt to examine this aspect of potting technology there.

Unfortunately neither the Bicester Fields Farm nor the Slade Farm assemblage was able to add anything to the somewhat vexed question of the chronology of the introduction of 'Belgic type' technology into the region, though the lack of wheel-thrown material at Bicester Fields Farm makes it clear that adoption of the new 'package' could be partial. From the perspective of sites further west in the region a date no more than a generation before the Roman conquest still seems likely for the introduction of grog-tempered traditions (e.g. Booth 1997b: 81-2). At present there is no evidence for or against the proposition that this introduction could have occurred slightly earlier in eastern Oxfordshire - given that this area can probably be attributed to the Catuvellauni rather than the Dobunni of the Upper Thames.

At Aves Ditch the pottery recovered from the bank, and thus providing a *terminus post quem* for its construction, seems to have been consistently of middle Iron Age character. In the 1997-98 trenches late Iron Age material was almost entirely absent, but its presence, as with that of any other material, would be dependent upon the occurrence of enough activity in the immediate area to generate rubbish. From the 1937 excavation, however, it seems that the early fills of the ditch produced consistently late Iron Age material, with the exception of a single small early Roman sherd (in fabric F25) from trench II. As it is not from the primary silt in the ditch, but from amongst the large stones above it, deriving almost certainly from the bank, it provides no more than a likely *terminus ante quem* for the start of significant re-deposition of bank material into the ditch. The late Iron Age sherds do not themselves date the construction of Aves Ditch, but they may be indicative of the date of the early phases of its use.

Material of middle and late Iron Age date was recovered from deposits predating and within the bank of the South Oxfordshire Grim's Ditch just east of Wallingford (Booth forthcoming) as well as from the early fills of the associated ditch. The general character of this material was very similar to that of the Aves Ditch assemblage, with a low average sherd weight (pre Grim's Ditch contexts produced 14 sherds (62 g) and the 26 sherds associated with the bank and early ditch fills weighed 178 g; an overall mean weight of 6 g). Given the general similarities in character between Aves Ditch and the South Oxfordshire Grim's Ditch the ceramic material associated with the latter may be a guide to the date of the former, although strictly the evidence from Aves Ditch, while potentially entirely consistent with this dating, is not as closely defined. Further parallels are found in the context of the North Oxfordshire Grim's Ditch, where 'Belgic type' pottery has been found sealed by and incorporated within the banks of the Grim's Ditch near Ditchley (Harden 1937: 80), near North Lodge, Blenheim Park (*ibid.*: 82-3) and at Callow Hill (Thomas 1958: 32-4).

Catalogue

Key to dates:

EIA/MIA	Early/ mid Iron Age
MIA	Mid Iron Age
Later MIA	Later Mid Iron Age
LIA/ERB	Late Iron Age or early Romano-British (i.e. prob. AD 20-50 or poss. AD 1-70)
ERB	Early Romano-British
RB	Romano-British
1-2C	1st to 2nd century AD
Late 1-2C	Late 1st to 2nd century AD
Late 1-3C	Late 1st to 3rd century AD
2C	2nd century AD
2-4C	2nd to 4th century AD
240-400	AD 240-400
Post-med	Post-medieval
?	date to specified period tentative

Table 3: 1997-98 Trench 1 by pottery small find number (see **fig. 16**)

Pot number	Context	3D: E of NW-peg/ S of profile line (-x = N of profile line)/ height above sea-level in metres	No. sherds	Wt (g)	Date (*terminus post quem*)	Fabric/ Comment
P1/1-2	U/S	-				Charcoal
P1/1	23	12.40/ 0.78/ 107.94	1	6	MIA	AS3
P1/1	23	As above	12	80	MIA	CVS3
P1/1	23	As above	1	4	MIA	CVS3 (C rim 113)
P2/1	2 or 19	-	1	1	MIA	AV3; + 1 frag not pot
P3/1	23	11.81/ 1.10/ 107.91	1	4	MIA	CV3
P4/1	23	11.90/ c. 1.12/ 107.86	3	22	MIA	CV3
P5/1	U/S, prob. bank	-	1	2	MIA	AV3
P6/1	23	11.75/ 1.20/ 107.97	2	6	MIA	CV3
P7/1	2	13.07/ 1.11/ 109.28	1	4	MIA	AV3
P8/1	2	11.52/ 0.95/ 109.30	1	4	MIA	AV3
P9/1	2	12.96/ 1.24/ 109.31	2	14	MIA	AVS3
P10/1	8C	6.26/ 1.13/ 107.545	1	12	?MIA	SN4
P11/1	8C	6.62/ 1.65/ 107.61	1	6	?Late 1-2C	W20 (?E - no rim)
P12/1	8B	7.29/ -0.59/ 107.92	1	4	?1-2C	SN4/C10
P13/1	8C	6.50/ 1.61/ 107.705	1	12	?Late 1-2C	R37 (D rim)
P14/1	2	11.43/ -/ c. 109.84	1	6	MIA	AVS3
P15/1	9D	6.17/ 1.35/ 107.39	1	10	LIA/ERB	GA3/E80
P16/1	3	11.75-11.95/ 0.60-0.70/ c. 108.98-109.09	1	1	MIA	CA3
P17/1	8C	5.97/ 1.60/ 107.63	1	4	MIA	LA4
P18/1	15	9.90/ c. 0.82-0.87/ 109.145	1	8	Later MIA	AVSG3 same as P22/1
P19/1	5A	12.94/ 0.38/ c. 109.02	1	14	MIA	AV3
P20/1	3	11.565/ 0.59/ c. 108.97	1	2	MIA	ALV3
P21/1	23	11.32/ 0.90/ 107.785	1	24	MIA	CS3 base
P22/1	15	10.28/ -/ c. 109.54	1	24	Later MIA	AVSG3 same as P18/1
P23/1	3	Close to P20/1	1	4	MIA	ALV4
P24/1	U/S	-	1	6	MIA	CZ3
P25/1	U/S	-				Coal/clinker
P26/1	23	12.95/ 0.64/ 107.90				Not pot
P27/1	3	11.53/ 1.07/ 109.04	1	4	MIA	AV3
P28/1	3 or U/S?	? c. 10.90/ c. 1.24/ c. 109.25 – found whilst cutting back profile – not plotted	1	4	MIA	SV4
P29/1	8A	5.74/ 1.48/ 107.525	1	2	MIA	CS4
P30/1	23	12.95/ 0.64/ 107.91	1	28	MIA	SL4

Table 4: 1998 Trench 2 by pottery small find number (see **fig. 16**)

Pot number	Context	3D: E of NW-peg/ S of profile line/ height above sea-level in metres	No. sherds	Wt (g)	Date (*terminus post quem*)	Fabric/Comment
P1/2	34	16.28/ 0.50/ 108.50	1	3	MIA	CV4
P2/2	35	16.55/ 1.43/ 108.13	2	24	Later MIA	AG3
P3/2	U/S, prob. 35, 36 or 37	-	1	14	MIA	LSA4 (C rim 122)
P4/2	31	17.80/ 1.01/ 108.86	2	10	MIA	CZ3 + 1 frag stone
P5/2	30	16.72/ 0.34/ c. 109.13	1	4	MIA	CN4
P6/2	31	-/ -/ 108.705	1	4	MIA	AV3
P7/2	25	-				Limestone + 1 frag coal
P8/2	24	17.40/ 0.20/ c. 109.49				Coal
P9/2	24	-				Coal
P10/2	34	16.38/ 0.73/ 108.50	1	1	?MIA	CV4
P11/2	31	17.04/ 0.94/ 108.71	1	2	MIA	AV3
P12/2	31	16.525/ 0.83/ 108.86	4	11	MIA	CN3
P13/2	31	16.93/ 0.72/ 108.73	1	10	?MIA	AV3 (poss also some grog?)
P14/2	31	17.66/ 0.95/ 108.92	1	4	MIA	CA3
P15/2	31	16.85/ 1.26/ 108.715	1	3	MIA	CN3
P16/2	36	17.10/ 1.37/ 108.15	1	3	MIA	AV3
P17/2	31	17.75/ 0.63/ 108.74	1	2	MIA	CN4
P18/2	34, 35, 36 or 37	-	1	10	Later MIA	AG3
P19/2	36	16.70/ 1.30/ 108.04	1	3	EIA/MIA	SA5
P20/2	36	17.39/ 1.29/ 108.04	1	6	MIA	LZ4
P21/2	31	16.24/ 0.95/ 108.87	1	10	?MIA	CSAV4
P22/2	35 or 36	16.90/ 1.18/ 108.20	1	2	MIA	CV3
P22/2	As above	As above	1	4	MIA	AL3 (C rim 113)
P23/2	31	16.35/ 0.38/ 108.84	1	3	MIA	CV3
P24/2	31	17.49/ 0.72/ 108.59				Limestone
P25/2	35	-	1	<1	MIA	ACV3
P26/2	U/S	-	2	1	?MIA	LS4

Table 5: 1997-98 Trench 1 context pottery dates

Context	No. sherds	Wt (g)	Date (*terminus post quem*)	Comment
US	2	8	MIA	
2	5	28	MIA	
2 or 19	1	1	MIA	
3	4	11	MIA	
3 or U/S	1	4	MIA	
5A	1	14	MIA	
8A	1	2	MIA	
8B	1	4	?1-2C	
8C	4	34	?Late 1-2C	2 sherds MIA
9D	1	10	LIA/ERB	
15	2	32	Later MIA	
23	22	174	MIA	1 rim

Table 6: 1998 Trench 2 context pottery dates

Context	No. sherds	Wt (g)	Date (*terminus post quem*)	Comment
US	2	1	?MIA	
US, prob. 35, 36 or 37	1	14	MIA	
30	1	4	MIA	
31	14	59	MIA	
34	2	4	MIA	
35	3	25	Later MIA	
35 or 36	2	6	MIA	1 rim
35, 36 or 37	1	10	Later MIA	same fabric as a sherd certainly from context 35
36	3	12	MIA	

Table 7: 1937 Trench I by pottery small find number (see **fig. 23**)

Ref no.	No. sherds	Wt (g)	Date (*terminus post quem*)	Comment
1	1	1		
2				Missing
3				Limestone
4	1	1	?LIA/ERB	
5	2	1	?LIA/ERB	
6	2	3	?LIA/ERB	
7	1	2	?LIA/ERB	
8	1	1	?LIA/ERB	
9	1	2	?LIA/ERB	
10	1	1		
11	2	2		
12	1	1		
13	1	4		
14	3	<1		
15	1	5	LIA/ERB	
16				Flint
17				Limestone and flint frags
18	1	1	?LIA/ERB	
19	1	3	RB	Plus 12 fragment (12 g) post-medieval tile

Table 8: 1937 Trench II by pottery small find number (see **fig. 23**)

Ref no.	No. sherds	Wt (g)	Date (*terminus post quem*)	Comment
20	2	4		
21	1	5	LIA/ERB	'?in earth bank just E of edge of stony bank'
22	2	1		
23	1	1		
24	1	2		
25	1	1		
26	1	1		
27	1	3		
28	1	1	LIA/ERB	
29	1	<1	LIA/ERB	
30	1	1		
31	1	1	?LIA/ERB	
32	1	1	LIA/ERB	Rim
33				Flint
34	1	3	ERB	Glazed sherd (F25)
35	1	1	LIA/ERB	
36				Limestone
37	1	3	?RB	
38	1	15	2-4 C	
39	1	8	Late 1-3 C	'from S end of stony bank depth unknown'
40	1	3	?Late 1-2 C	'from dump from fill of ditch'

Table 9: 1937 Trench III by pottery small find number (see **fig. 23**)

Ref no.	No. sherds	Wt (g)	Date (*terminus post quem*)	Comment
41	1	8	240-400	
42				2 frags (20 g) post-medieval tile
43	1	35	Post-med	plus 1 frag (35 g) post-medieval tile
44	2	28	Late 1-2C	
45	1	12	?Late 1-2C	
46	1	7	Late 1-3C	
47	1	<1	2C	CG samian
48	2	3	?Late 1-2C	

Table 10: 1937 Miscellaneous sherds

Ref no.	No. sherds	Wt (g)	Date (*terminus post quem*)	Comment
	1	1	?1-2 C	'from trial hole 20yds S of W end of trench I'
	4	13	?LIA/ERB	'23.3.37 on end of bank'

Archaeomagnetic dating At Aves Ditch
(see **fig. 40**)

by Patrick Erwin

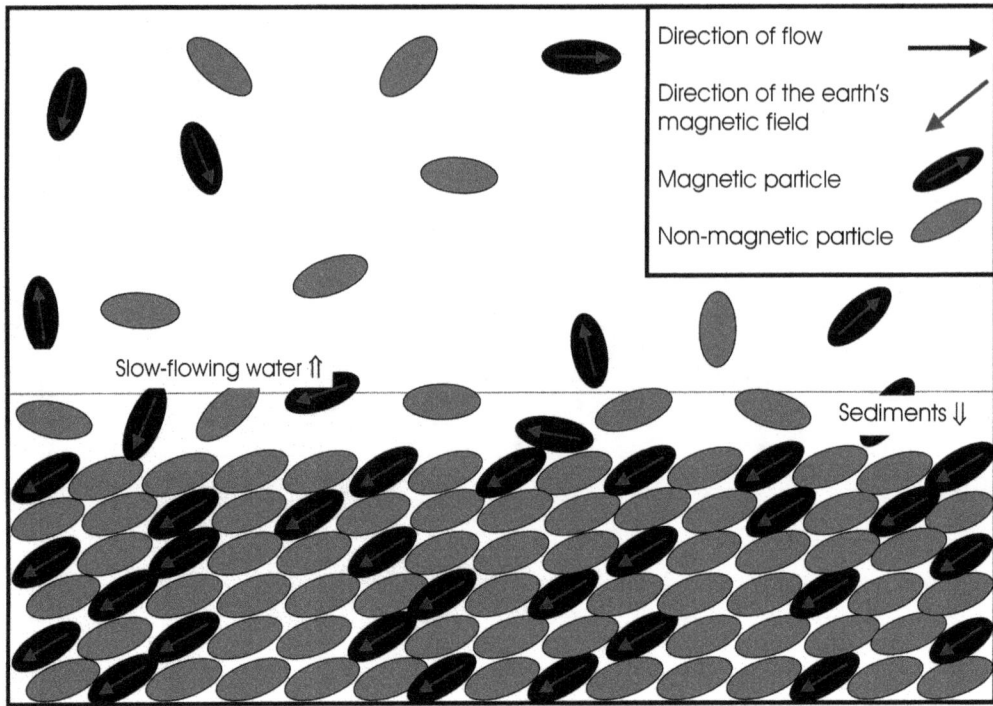

Figure 40. Principles of archaeomagnetic dating: when fine sediments containing magnetic minerals are deposited by slow flowing water, magnetic particles will tend to orientate themselves towards the earth's magnetic field. Hence when the water-borne sediments are deposited, these magnetic minerals record the direction of the geomagnetic field at the time of deposition. As the direction and intensity of the earth's magnetic field has been changing over time, if an orientated *in situ* sample can be taken, its magnetic record can be used for dating purposes.

Sampling at Aves Ditch (cf. Erwin 1999a and b) was extremely difficult due to the nature of the sediment (silty clay matrix with a high proportion of limestone fragments). However, between 10 and 16 oriented samples were collected from each of three contexts. The direction of remanence from each sample was determined through stepwise alternating field demagnetisation (10 steps) with remanence measured using a 2-axis CCL cryogenic magnetometer. Lines were fitted to this data for each point using the LINEFIND routine of Kent *et al.* (1983). These directions were then corrected to Meriden (52.43°N, 1.64°W), using the Noel and Batt (1990) method via pole.

For each context a vector average of directions was taken and an α95 calculated. This information was then plotted onto the calibration curve of Batt (1997) and estimates of the dates made (see table 11).

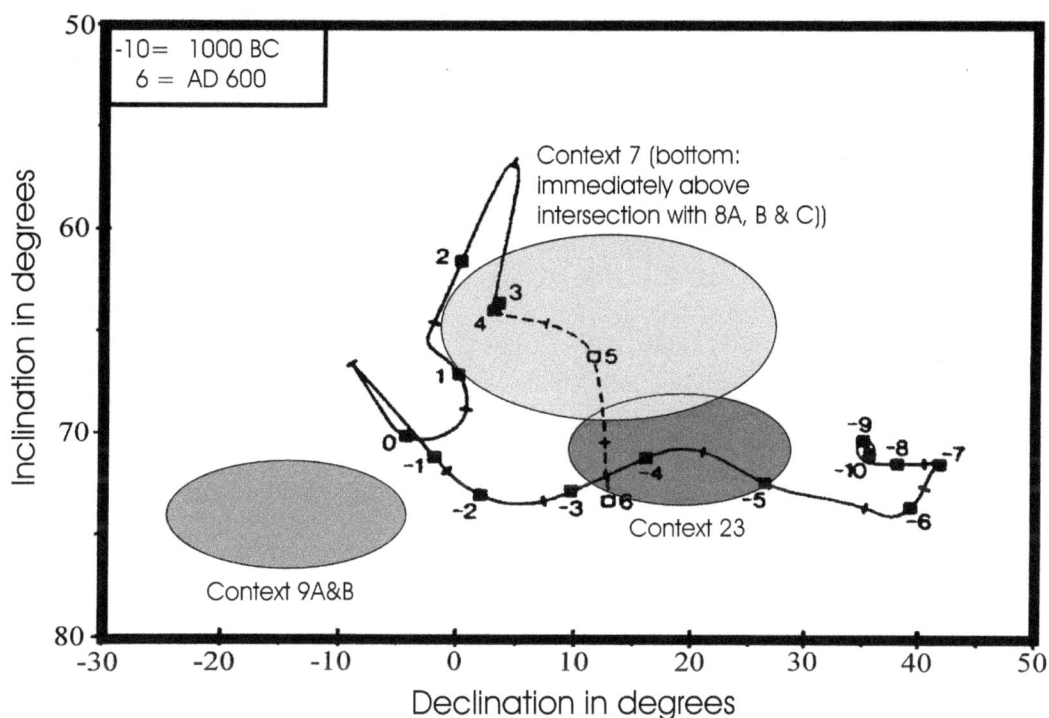

Figure 41. Declination and inclination of the archaeomagnetic samples from Aves Ditch in relation to the calibration curve.

Table 11: Archaeomagnetic dates from Aves Ditch (cf. **figs 16 and 41**). The 'No.' refers to samples exhibiting a measurable remnant magnetisation.

Context	No.	Dec.	Inc.	α95	Date range
7*	6	13.0	65.3	11.6	AD 275-550
9A/B	10	-34.5	74.0	5.0	250 BC?-AD150? (off curve)
23	11	15.3	71.8	6.1	500-325 BC

* Bottom of context (see **fig. 16**)

The conditions on this site were far from ideal for archaeomagnetic dating, so some caution must be used in the interpretation of these dates. However, the archaeomagnetic evidence suggests a late Iron Age to early Roman date for the earliest sedimentation in the 'main' Aves Ditch. The underlying curving ditch is dated to 500-325BC. The silt accumulating at the bottom of context 7 (which is immediately above the grave cut, though none of the samples were taken from above the grave, but to the north and south of the burial) appears to have accumulated between AD 275 and 550.

The Coin

by Eberhard W. Sauer

A coin of 2.229 g weight and 15 x 17 mm diameter was found in 1998 in trench 2 (**fig. 16**; context 30, 3D: 16.17 E/ 0.26 S/ 109.22 m above sea-level). Its extremely poor preservation allowed no certain identification, neither before nor after cleaning by Dr Graham Morgan. Possible signs of a central head were observed, and there are faint traces of lettering on the same side (the obverse?) around the rim, which may read: '[---]VA[---]'. If so, an attribution to the reigns of Valens or Valentinian I. or II, i.e. to AD 364-392, is the most likely, but not the only, solution. The module and appearance leave in any case little doubt that it is a late Roman piece, datable to c. AD 260-400. The post-Roman glass fragment (see Hoffmann below) suggests that the coin was re-deposited at a much later date. These finds suggest that there was a considerable built-up of deposits on the east side of Aves Ditch in the post-Roman period and that, while the curving ditch may have been largely filled up in the Iron Age, much of the Iron Age pottery from higher levels was re-deposited in the medieval or modern period.

The glass fragment

by Birgitta Hoffmann

Other than from the uppermost fill of Aves Ditch, only one fragment of glass was found in the 1997/98 excavation. It derives from immediately above the fill of the curving ditch in a section behind, and not sealed by, the bank of Aves Ditch (**fig. 16**; context 31, 3D: 16.97 E/ 0.39 S/ 108.61 m above sea-level). It thus provides no *terminus post quem* for the earthwork, only for the deposits above it in trench 2.

The piece is a dark olive green body fragment with a series of parallel weathering lines. The shape of the fragment suggests a cylindrical vessel with a curved base or shoulder. The colour is consistent with sixth to eighth-century AD fragments from Anglo-Saxon settlement sites. However, vessels of the same colour were produced in large quantities in the early modern period. This makes it, disregarding the archaeological context, numerically much more likely that this comes from an early modern vessel, such as a small bottle. But the weathering on the surface in fine line is not common on modern vessels.

In the absence of other Anglo-Saxon artefacts from the immediate vicinity, a final decision as to whether it is Anglo-Saxon or modern cannot be made.

HUMAN BONES
(see **figs 13, 16 and 32-35**)

by Peter Hacking

At the time of the excavation in 1997 the unexpected finding of bone resulted in the collection of many broken fragments. Nevertheless it was possible to reassemble a proportion of the pieces of long bone cortex and recognise the mid-shafts of both femora, tibiae and fibulae - more than sufficient to identify the bones as being those of a human adult. With the exception of one fragment the bones around the knees had been lost. Although broken the bones were well preserved and from their robusticity a male skeleton was suggested. One finger bone was the only intact finding.

Careful re-excavation in 1998 revealed an almost complete skeleton from the level of the pelvis and upper femora upwards including the vertebrae from CV2 (the axis) in the neck down to the end of the sacrum, the ribs, the shoulder girdles, arms and hands, the pelvis and hips.

What was most striking was that, although all of the mandible, though broken, was present, the atlas (CV1) and the whole of the skull appeared to be missing; just one fragment of the cranial vault, measuring 30x40mm and with one sutural edge, was found a short distance away from its expected site.

It was now possible to assess the sex and age and estimate the stature of the individual. Sex was assessed using the criteria of the Workshop of European Anthropologists (1980); all the pelvic features - narrow sciatic notches and subpubic angle, strongly everted ischiopubic rami and absent preauricular sulci indicate a male, as does the length of the intact right clavicle (>150mm) and the diameters (50mm) of the femoral and humeral heads. Age assessment was made from the degree of attrition of the lower molar teeth according to Brothwell's (1981) criteria, indicating approximately 35 years; this was supported by the appearance of the pubic symphyses (35-39 years), (Suchey & Brooks,1990) and the anterior ends of several ribs (c.30 years), (Iscan *et al.* 1984).

The estimate of stature is best made from measurements of the lengths of the leg bones but this was impossible, none of the these bones being complete; only the lengths of the right humerus and the left radius were measurable; using the formulae of Trotter & Gleser (1958), a height of 1.74 m is suggested but this must be regarded only as an approximation.

The bones do not show any evidence of severe pathology and certainly no evidence of the cause of death; a minor degree of osteophytic lipping (bony spur formation) on several mid-vertebral bodies, and on the margins of the hips, shoulders and wrists are stress-related and suggest that he had been used to performing considerable physical work.

The presence of the mandible - and the absence of any cut marks on the skull fragment, the mandible and on any of the cervical vertebrae - suggests that the skull was removed only after some decomposition had occurred. The atlas (CV1) was not recovered, suggesting that it had remained attached to the base of the skull. As a rule decapitation either at execution or shortly after death occurs at the level of CV3 or 4 (Harman *et al.* 1981); here, although CV3 was incomplete (the neural arch was present, but the vertebral body was not found), CV4 did not show any damage. The finding of one fragment of the vault remains enigmatic, but must indicate some damage occurring during removal.

ANIMAL BONES

by Stephanie Knight

Introduction

The recovered animal bone from the Aves Ditch excavations 1997-1998 was in relatively poor condition: bone was often fragmented, with only six complete bones from a total of 238 (2.5%). The bone which was complete was often not measurable due to the high incidence of root damage (151 examples or 63.4%), and it is probable that the badly eroded surface of the bone masked other taphonomic effects, such as gnawing (with 5 examples or 2.1%) and butchery (2 examples, or 0.8%). The fragmentation and poor condition of bone will have contributed to the low identification rate (145 or 60.9% unidentified).

Modern fractures were noted on 15 examples, or 6.3% of the assemblage, probably resulting from the methods of excavation in the bank and curving ditch, which were excavated by mattock. In the area of the human burial, trowels and leaf tools were used.

Sieving of deposits was not carried out, other than for one soil sample each per key deposit, none of which yielded any animal bones, and the recovery rate of small bones, such as sheep phalanges and bird bones, may thus be lower than had the excavation strategy involved sieving of a larger proportion of the soil. However, poor bone preservation may also have contributed to any deficiency of small bone in the assemblage.

Bone was recovered from the bank of Aves Ditch, from an earlier curving ditch (**fig. 13**, almost certainly associated with an Iron Age enclosure [**fig. 14**]) and from the area of a burial of a c. 35 year old male, situated in the ditch of the linear earthwork. Bone in the rampart may have been re-deposited from an earlier enclosure. Table 12 gives the number of recovered fragments in full, but for further analysis the faunal remains were divided into three context groups (the bank of Aves Ditch, the curving ditch and the burial/ main ditch), since the number of identified bone was too small in some contexts for individual analysis.

Table 12: Animal bone from Aves Ditch: total fragment count

Species	Bone count	Bank			Curving ditch	Burial/ main ditch	Bank or curving ditch	Total	Un-stratified
		upper	lower	total					
Cattle	Fragment No.	5	5	10	20	3	3	36	1
	Epiphyses only	*0*	*4*	*4*	*6*	*1*	*0*	*11*	*0*
	MNI	*1*	*1*	*1*	*2*	*1*	*1*	*2*	
Sheep/ Goat	Fragment No.	0	4	4	31	2	5	42	3
	Epiphyses only	*0*	*0*	*0*	*7*	*0*	*1*	*8*	*0*
	MNI	*0*	*1*	*1*	*2*	*1*	*1*	*2*	
Pig	Fragment No.	0	0	0	6	0	0	6	0
	Epiphyses only	*0*	*0*	*0*	*1*	*0*	*0*	*1*	*0*
	MNI	*0*	*0*	*0*	*1*	*0*	*0*	*1*	
Horse	Fragment No.	0	1	1	3	0	1	5	0
	Epiphyses only	*0*	*0*	*0*	*3*	*0*	*1*	*4*	*0*
	MNI	*0*	*1*	*1*	*1*	*0*	*1*	*1*	
Unidentified	Fragment No.	7	23	30	89	4	11	134	11
Total	Fragment No.	12	33	45	149	9	20	223	15

No goat bone was identified in the assemblage, but this does not necessarily mean that goat was absent, since the poor condition of the bone would have obscured any defining characteristics between ovine and caprine. Here all references to sheep indicate sheep *or* goat bone.

The fragmented nature of this assemblage suggests that looking at fragment numbers to determine species proportions would lead to over-representation of the larger species, which break into more recognisable parts. Thus the epiphyses-only method (Grant 1975), counting selected parts of bones so as to avoid repetition of broken elements, is also used here, as well as using the minimum number of individuals. These may be more appropriate, as they filter out bias introduced by more fragmented bones and by teeth, which are numerous, survive well and can easily fall out of the jaw. The total numbers by context are too small for the MNI count to be particularly useful here.

Species proportions

Table 13: Species proportions in percentages (using three methods of analysis)

Species	Cattle			Sheep/ Goat			Pig			Horse		
Feature	**Frag**	*Epiph*	MNI	**Frag**	*Epiph*	MNI	**Frag**	*Epiph*	MNI	**Frag**	*Epiph*	MNI
Bank	66.7	100.0	33.3	26.7	0	33.3	0	0	0	6.7	0	33.3
Curving ditch	33.3	35.3	33.3	51.7	41.2	33.3	10.0	5.9	16.7	5.0	17.6	16.7
Burial/ main ditch	60.0	100.0	50.0	40.0	0	50.0	0	0	0	0	0	0
Total	40.4	45.8	33.3	47.2	33.3	33.3	6.7	4.2	16.7	5.6	16.7	16.7

By fragment count, sheep are most common at 47.2%, followed by cattle (40.4%) then pig (6.7%) and horse (5.6%). Epiphyses-only counts give a higher percentage for cattle and horse than fragment count, while sheep are less well represented. The greater proportion of cattle seen when using the epiphyses-only method suggests that the sheep bones in fact suffered from a greater degree of fragmentation, and that cattle bones were the most common at the site overall.

When using a minimum number of individuals count, sheep and cattle are equally represented and pig and horse less common, each pair showing the same proportions. Using MNI analysis, however, is not suited to such small samples.

Individually, the contexts show different proportions of species to each other, although the differences are likely to be due mainly to small sample size. This is especially true of the area around the burial (including some other bones from the main ditch), which shows only 9 examples of bone, of which only 2 were not fragments or teeth. Aves Ditch (including the area of the burial) shows different species proportions to the fill of the curving ditch: Aves Ditch (though the sample is too small to be statistically valid) has a majority of cattle bone, and the curving ditch a majority of sheep; in the curving ditch there is also evidence for a wider range of other species, including pig and horse (which, however, could be solely due to the sample size being over ten times greater).

The differences in species proportions shown between the curving ditch and the bank of Aves Ditch are evident, regardless of the method of analysis. Using a fragment count, cattle bone is more numerous in the bank of Aves Ditch (66.7%) than the curving ditch (33.3%), while sheep are less numerous (26.7% in the bank of Aves Ditch to 51.7% in the curving ditch). It appears that in the bank of Aves Ditch the larger animal is better represented, possibly indicating that it contains more fragmented material, which would comprise more recognisable parts of cattle bone than sheep. Using epiphyses-only counts, sheep are again less well represented in the bank of Aves Ditch (i.e. there is no certain sheep epiphysis), but have a greater representation than cattle in the curving ditch. This suggests that that bone was indeed less fragmented in the curving ditch. The rate of erosion in both is similar, at 80.0% in the bank of Aves Ditch and 68.8% in the curving ditch, indicating that greater fragmentation in the bank of Aves Ditch could have resulted from human activity rather than preservational difference.

The differences between the bank and the curving ditch may be significant, but the small numbers of bone from each make such a conclusion tenuous without further investigation.

Bone element analysis

The bone assemblage was initially analysed whole, since the numbers of epiphyses were very few. Only cattle, sheep and horse yielded multiple numbers of bone epiphyses: pig showed only one example (a pig tibia). The contents of individual contexts were also examined.

The elements on the left of the x-axis in **figs 42 and 43** are those which, taking into account density and size, would be expected to be best represented assuming there had been no differential dispersal of the carcass parts (Grant 1975: 384; 1984: 498). The bone percentages were calculated using the epiphyses-only counts to determine the best represented element; the relative frequency of other elements are displayed as a percentage of that count. Bones which are represented more than once in the skeleton have their counts reduced accordingly, i.e. divided by eight for cattle phalanges or divided by two for the distal humerus.

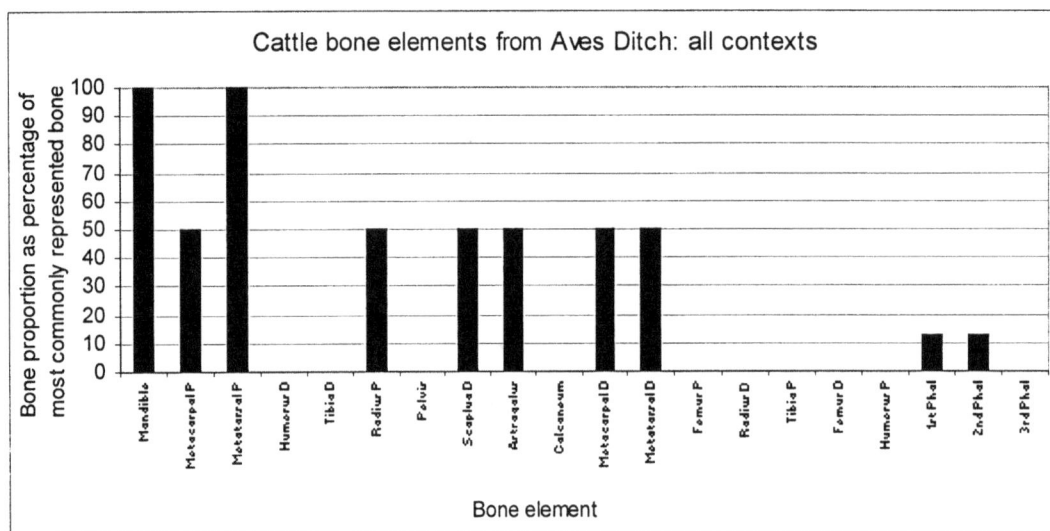

Figure 42. Cattle bone elements from the Aves Ditch excavations.

Cattle bone elements show the pattern expected from Brain's (1981) taphonomic observations, with more dense bones (shown on the left of the x-axis) and fewer of the more fragile elements (on the right). Not all bones are represented, but this is probably due to the small sample rather than to an absence caused by human behaviour: the most commonly represented bones (the mandible and proximal metatarsal) only show two examples of each. The bones which are represented do not show any patterns which could suggest human activity (for example selective consumption or trading of parts): they are from different parts of the carcass and not mainly either 'meat' or 'waste' bone. There is more 'waste' bone (head and foot) represented, but the presence of a scapula and radius as well suggests this is a mixed deposit.

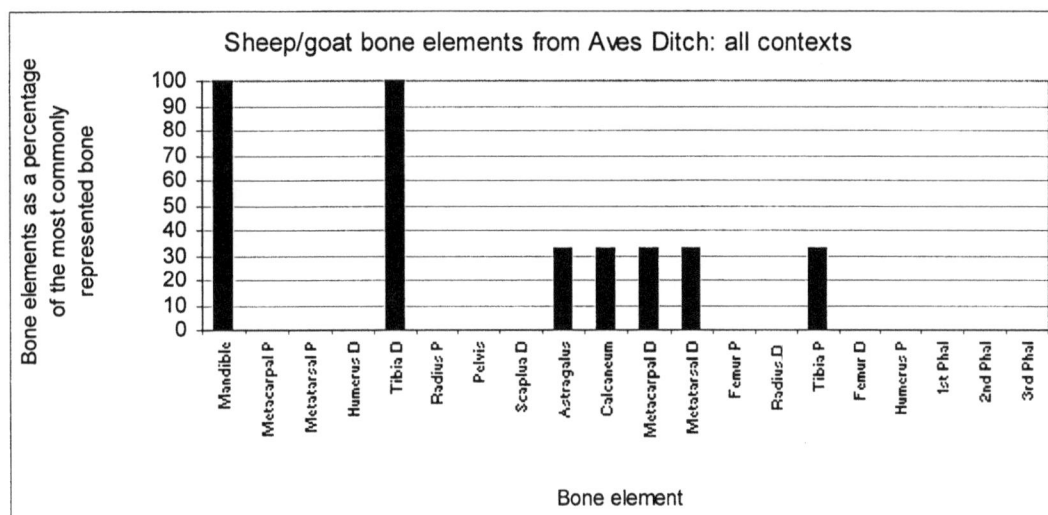

Figure 43. Sheep/ goat bone elements from the Aves Ditch excavations.

There were very few sheep bone epiphyses: **fig. 43** shows that the mandible and distal tibia were most common, but there were only three examples of each. The bone elements roughly follow the expected survival pattern, with the majority from 'waste' bones, but the small numbers of investigated bone mean that this is probably not significant.

When divided into feature types (in this case the bank of Aves Ditch, the curving ditch and the burial/ main ditch), there are so few examples that analysis is very difficult, but a brief synopsis is presented below.

The bone from the area of the burial consists of elements which do not carry a large amount of meat: a fragment of a cattle tibia and first phalange, a few unidentified fragments probably from the cattle tibia, and a sheep tooth, which may have been incorporated by chance. It is not what could be identified as the remains of a burial feast or a ritual deposit (Grant 1984: 533), which is in keeping with Sauer's interpretation of the body as 'unloved dead' (Sauer 1999b: 269) with no grave goods. The bone from this area appears to have been incorporated by chance rather than as an offering or specific deposit.

The bone from the bank of Aves Ditch also contains a lower proportion of meat-bearing than 'waste' bones. However, the bone from the curving ditch includes cattle head and feet bone and fragments from cattle humerus and tibia, sheep head, feet, upper and lower limb bone and a vertebral fragment, and a pig tibia and scapula. There is a mixture of species and bone elements from the curving ditch, which includes bone from all main parts of the carcass: head, foot, torso, fore and hind limbs.

The small numbers of bones recovered do not allow for major conclusions to be drawn, and no significant differences can be identified between the bones from these different deposits.

Husbandry methods: age at death using toothwear and bone fusion analysis

The number of bone recovered is too small for a detailed analysis of the age structure of animals by species. Toothwear from only four sheep mandibles could be measured, and none of them provided complete molar rows, so Mandibular Wear Stages as defined by Grant (1982) could not be given.

Bone fusion analysis, using data from Silver (1969), was also hampered by the small number of suitable examples: only 18 epiphyses from all species could be aged.

Eight cattle bones were fused, including a scapula (which fuses at 7-8 months) and a distal metatarsal (fusing at 27-36 months). These bones may have all come from one animal, and if so this animal was over the age of 27 months at death, and so was probably a relatively mature animal which may have been kept for milk or traction, rather than as a meat source.

Table 14: Fusion status of sheep bone: all contexts

Bone Element	Age at Fusion	Fusion Status
First Phalange	13-16 months	Recently fused
Tibia D	18-24 months	Unfused (2)
Metacarpal D	18-24 months	Fused
Metatarsal D	20-28 months	Unfused
Calcaneum	30-36 months	Unfused

Of the sheep bones, however, most were unfused. Table 14 indicates that the recovered sheep bone was from at least two individuals, one of which died at or before the age of 18 months (shown by the unfused distal tibiae), and the other at or before 28 months (shown by an unfused distal metatarsal). The fused distal metacarpal indicates that one individual lived to over 18 months at least. Silver's figures are from modern breeds which probably mature earlier than 'unimproved' animals, so it is likely that the two sheep represented here were younger than the modern figures suggest. One at least was killed relatively young, suggesting that the flock could have been kept for meat and milk production, not necessarily for wool.

A fused distal pig tibia from the curving ditch indicated an animal that died when aged over 24 months, a relatively mature individual, considering that modern pigs mature at or under the age of 1 year, although unimproved breeds mature later.

Butchery

Only one definite butchery mark was recorded, although many more may have been obscured by erosion of the bone surface. A cattle metatarsal shows transverse marks across the shaft, possibly created during skinning. A cattle scapula may have been chopped through at the neck, although erosion on the surface did not allow firm identification of this as a chop mark.

Measurements

Of the bone which had complete epiphyses, most were eroded and only three were in a suitable state of preservation to be measured. These were measured according to von den Driesch and Boessneck (1974) and the results are given in table 15.

Table 15: Bone measurements from Aves Ditch

Species	Bone	Measurement	Reading in mm
Cattle	first phalange	proximal width	28.0
Cattle	metatarsal	distal width	51.4
Pig	tibia	distal width	21.1

No withers heights could be estimated from these measurements, but the cattle metatarsal measurement fits into the range of this bone from Danebury (44-59mm), although the distal width of the pig tibia is smaller than those from Danebury (25-32 mm) (Grant 1984).

Conclusions

The poor condition of the assemblage, caused by erosion and fragmentation, together with a small sample size, limited the detail in which the assemblage could be studied. Information on butchery and size of the animals was very restricted. A count of fragments showed sheep to be predominant, followed by cattle, pig and horse, but a restricted (epiphyses-only) bone count showed cattle to be more common than sheep, followed by horse and pig (tables 12 and 13).

No differences could be determined between feature types, although there was slightly more evidence for fragmentation and over-representation of cattle in the bank of Aves Ditch than in the curving ditch. There was also a slightly lower proportion of 'meaty' bone in the Aves Ditch bank, although both of these effects could have been due to the small sample size and fragmentation through reworking of deposits, rather than deliberate human activity, such as the inclusion of primary butchery waste in the bank material. There was no evidence of a different type of deposit around the burial.

A minimum of one immature and one sheep/ goat over the age of 18 months was present, one mature pig and one mature horse were also represented, while cattle were skeletally mature. The animal ages were generally consistent with another Iron Age site at Danebury (Grant 1984: 503-520), apart from the pig which was older at death than most pigs from Danebury.

Butchery marks on cattle bone suggested cattle had been skinned and possibly chopped, much like those from Danebury (Knight 2003). Measurements showed that the pig was possibly a smaller animal than those from Danebury, maybe that it was a female or different breed, but the cattle were of a similar size.

The species proportions and husbandry patterns implied by the animal bone from Aves Ditch thus seem to be typical of Iron Age faunal assemblages in this area (Maltby 1981). Butchery and animal size also seem to be comparable, although pigs from the curving ditch assemblage may have been smaller than those from Danebury. The curving ditch is earlier than Aves Ditch and its bank, and thus differences are possible between them. However, the bank is likely to contain a significant proportion of re-deposited material from the enclosure (**fig. 14**), thought to be associated with the curving ditch. These differences might include the presence of less meaty parts and more cattle in the bank of Aves Ditch, although it is important to remember that the sample size is small and that only a small section of the bank and ditches has been excavated.

LAND SNAILS FROM AVES DITCH

by Mark Robinson

Four samples were analysed for lands snails from the 1997/98 trenches 1 and 2 across Aves Ditch. The deposits investigated were Contexts 23 and 36, pale reddish brown silt loam with small limestone fragments filling an Iron Age ditch sealed beneath the bank of Aves Ditch, and Contexts 9A and 9B/C, reddish brown silt loam with secondary carbonate deposits and limestone fragments at the bottom of the Aves Ditch on either side. Samples of 1kg were sieved over a 0.5mm mesh, sorted for shells and the results listed in Table 16. Three samples contained useful quantities of shells. Context 36 only contained shell fragments of *Cepaea* sp.

The snails from Context 23 were species of dry open habitats, such as *Vallonia costata* and *Helicella itala*. They suggested that the Iron Age enclosure was set within a cleared landscape.

The snails from Contexts 9A and 9B/C included both species of open habitats, such as *Pupilla muscorum* and *H. itala*, and species of shaded habitats including *Carychium tridentatum* and *Vitrea* sp. Some snails will live in the interstices between fragments of limestone but the assemblages were not rock-rubble faunas. These results suggested either that tall vegetation grew in the ditch or that there was some scrub near the ditch. It is possible there was a hedge alongside Aves Ditch.

Table 16: Land snails from Aves Ditch

	Min. no. indiv.		
Context (cf. fig. 16)	**23**	**9A**	**9B/C**
Carychium tridentatum	-	4	10
Cochlicopa sp.	-	2	-
Vertigo pygmaea	-	1	-
Pupilla muscorum	2	3	-
Vallonia costata	4	2	2
Vallonia excentrica	-	-	1
Vallonia sp.	5	1	1
Acanthinula aculeata	-	-	1
Discus rotundatus	-	-	1
Vitrina sp.	1	-	-
Vitrea sp.	-	3	2
Nesovitrea hammonis	-	-	1
Aegopinella nitidula	-	-	1
Limax or *Deroceras* sp.	-	1	2
Helicella itala	2	4	3
Cepaea sp.	1	1	-
Total	**15**	**22**	**25**

ACKNOWLEDGEMENTS

I am indebted to Mr and Mrs Norman for their kind permission to excavate and their interest and support. I am grateful to the Administrators of the Haverfield Bequest, the Council of British Archaeology and the Oxford University Archaeological Society for funding the fieldwork, to the Leicester University Research Fund for providing a grant for specialists' reports, to NERC for one radiocarbon date via the NERC-ORADS radiocarbon dating programme, to the British Archaeological Research Trust for another and to Dr Tom Higham of Oxford University's RLAHA for carrying out the dating. I would like to acknowledge further support by Edinburgh University's School of History and Classics, where I am based now and where the report has been written, and by the staff of the University's Graphics and Multimedia Resource Centre and of various libraries.

The partially physically demanding and partially delicate work, ranging from a deep section through a stone bank to the excavation of a human burial, could not have taken place without the dedicated support of members of the Oxford University Archaeology Society and other volunteers; space allows me to name only a few: Maricel Acevedo, Annouchka Bayley, Dr Ian Brown, Tim Bryars, Simon Chadwick, Jennifer Emmett, Dr Patrick Erwin, Dr Avi Faust, Dr Simon Heap, Dr Richard Lewis, Jonathan Lowther, Hywel Luff, Emma Smith, Bernd Sprenzel, Marcus Starling, Terry Stopps, Yuko Takigawa, Jeffrey Wallis, Carole Walton and William Whiteley.

I would like to thank Professor Barry Cunliffe, Professor Richard Bradley, Dr Martin Henig and Professor Greg Woolf (then the OUAS senior member) for essential support of the project and Professor Don Scragg for advice on a translation from Anglo-Saxon to English. The book greatly benefited from the advice of Tim Bryars, Dr Patrick Erwin, Chris Green, Dr Peter Hacking and Dr Birgitta Hoffmann, who kindly read and commented on the entire report. They have all offered invaluable improvements to language and contents and eradicated numerous passages, which lacked clarity or substance, while they are not responsible for any remaining shortcomings. Alison Roberts of the Ashmolean Museum located the records and finds of the 1937 excavations, kindly made them available to us and allowed us to include them in this report. Several institutions granted permission to reproduce images, and their help is acknowledged in the picture legends. Simon Crutchley of English Heritage offered advice and valuable help on aerial photographs and other matters. Susan Lisk and Paul Smith provided access to the Oxfordshire SMR, Philip Tallon drew my attention to his research on the place name evidence and members of Cotswold Archaeology kindly showed me their excavations near the Gorse on 21 June 2005. To Dr David Davison I am not only grateful for accepting this report for publication, but also for his editorial support and the professional design at BAR, which exceeded all of my expectations. I am particularly indebted to all of my fellow authors, who have made crucial contributions to the success of the project, and most of them have even done so on a purely voluntary basis.

BIBLIOGRAPHY
(including classical and medieval sources and abbreviations)

Allen, T., 2000 'The Iron Age Background', in Henig and Booth 2000: 1-33.

Ammianus Marcellinus.

Angenendt, A., 1991 'Corpus incorruptum. Eine Leitidee der mittelalterlichen Reliquienver-ehrung.' *Saeculum* 42: 320-48.

Anon. 1842 *The Award of the Commissioner appointed to Inclose the Parish of Upper-Heyford*, 31/12/1842.

Anon. 1937 'Archaeological Notes 10. Aves Ditch, Kirtlington, Oxon.' *Oxoniensia* 2: 202.

Anon. 1938 'Roman Britain in 1937 I. Sites explored.' *Journal of Roman Studies* 28: 169-98.

Atkinson, R.J.C. and McKenzie, A., 1946-1947 'Archaeological Notes, 1946, 2. Aves Ditch, Oxon.' *Oxoniensia* 11-12: 162.

Avery, M., Sutton, J.E.G. and Banks, J.W., 1968 'Rainsborough, Northants, England: Excavations 1961-5.' *Proceedings of the Prehistoric Society*, New Ser. 33, for 1967: 207-306.

Ball, W. with Gardin, J.-C., 1982 *Archaeological Gazetteer of Afghanistan*, vols 1-2, Paris.

Ball, W., 2000 *Rome in the East. The transformation of an Empire*, London and New York.

Batt, C.M., 1997 'The British archaeomagnetic calibration curve an objective treatment.' *Archaeometry* 39: 153-68.

Bean, S.C., 2000 *The Coinage of the Atrebates and Regni*. University of Oxford: Committee for Archaeology Monograph 4, Oxford.

Beesley, A., 1841 *The History of Banbury*, London.

Bell, M., Fowler, P.J. and Hillson, S.W. (eds), 1996 *The Experimental Earthwork Project*. CBA Research Report 100, York.

Benoit, F., 1981 *Entremont, Capitale celto-ligure des Salyens de Provence*, Gap.

Benson, D. and Harding, D.W., 1968 'An Iron Age Site at Kirtlington, Oxon.' – 'Catalogue of the Pottery.' – 'The Pottery from Kirtlington, and its implications for the chronology of the earliest Iron Age in the Upper Thames Region.' *Oxoniensia* 31, for 1966: 157-61.

Berg, S., Rolle, R. and Seemann, H., 1981 *Der Archäologe und der Tod*, Munich and Luzern.

Bersu, G., Heimbs, G., Lange, H. and Schuchhardt, C., 1926 'Der Angrivarisch-Cheruskische Grenzwall und die beiden Schlachten des Jahres 16 nach Chr. zwischen Arminius und Germanicus.' *Praehistorische Zeitschrift* 17: 100-31.

Binder, J., 1924 *Heimatbuch für den Bezirk Leonberg*, Leonberg.

Bivar, A.D.H. and Fehérvári, G., 1966 'The Walls of Tammīsha.' *Iran* 4: 35-50.

Blair, J., 1994 *Anglo-Saxon Oxfordshire*, Stroud.

Blomfield, J.C., 1882. *History of the present deanery of Bicester, Oxon.*, Oxford and London.

Boon, G.C., 1976 'The Shrine of the Head, Caerwent', in Boon, G.C. and Lewis, J.M. (eds), *Welsh Antiquity*, Cardiff: 163-75.

Booth, P., 1997a *Asthall, Oxfordshire, excavations in a Roman 'small town', 1992*. Thames Valley Landscapes Monograph No. 9, Oxford.

Booth, P., 1997b 'Pottery and other ceramic finds', in Mould, C., An archaeological excavation at Oxford Road, Bicester, Oxfordshire. *Oxoniensia* 61, for 1996: 75-89.

Booth, P., 1998 'The Iron Age pottery', in Cropper, C. and Hardy, A., The excavation of Iron Age and medieval features at Glympton Park, Oxfordshire. *Oxoniensia* 62, for 1997: 104-7.

Booth, P., 2002 'Late Roman Cemeteries in Oxfordshire: a Review.' *Oxoniensia* 66, for 2001: 13-42.

Booth, P., forthcoming 'Grim's Ditch: Iron Age and Roman pottery', in Cromarty, A., Barclay, A. and Lambrick, G., *Settlement and landscape: the archaeology of the Wallingford Bypass*. Thames Valley Landscapes Monograph, Oxford.

Booth, P., Boyle, A., and Keevill, G.D., 1994 'A Romano-British kiln site at Lower Farm, Nuneham Courtenay, and other sites on the Didcot to Oxford and Wootton to Abingdon water mains, Oxfordshire.' *Oxoniensia* 58, for 1993: 87-217.

Booth, P.M., Evans, J. and Hiller, J., 2002 *Excavations in the Extramural Settlement of Roman Alchester, Oxfordshire, 1991.* Oxford Archaeology Monographs 1, Oxford.

Bosworth, J. and Toller, T.N., 1898 *An Anglo-Saxon Dictionary*, Oxford.

Bowen, H.C., 1990 *The Archaeology of Bokerley Dyke*, London.

Boyle, A., 2002 'Human Skeletal Assemblage', in Booth *et al.* 2002: 385-94.

Boylston, A., Knüsel, C.J. and Roberts, C.A., 2000 'Investigation of a Romano-British Rural Ritual in Bedford, England.' *Journal of Archaeological Science* 27: 241-54.

Bradley, R., 1969 'The South Oxfordshire Grim's Ditch and its Significance.' *Oxoniensia* 33, for 1968: 1-13.

Bradley, R., 1971 'A field survey of the Chichester entrenchments', in Cunliffe, B., *Excavations at Fishbourne 1961-1969.* Reports of the Research Committee of the Society of Antiquaries of London 26, London and Leeds: 17-36.

Bradley, R., 2000 *An Archaeology of Natural Places*, London and New York.

Bradley, R., Entwistle, R. and Raymond, F., 1994 *Prehistoric Land Divisions on Salisbury Plain. The work of the Wessex Linear Ditches Project.* English Heritage Archaeological Report 2, London.

Bradley, R. and Williams, H. (eds), 1998 *The Past in the Past: the Reuse of Ancient Monuments.* World Archaeology 30.1, Abingdon.

Brain, C., 1981 *The Hunters or the Hunted?*, Chicago.

Branigan, K., 1985 *The Catuvellauni*, Gloucester.

Brothwell, D., 1981 *Digging up bones,* 3rd edn, New York.

Brown, K., 2000 'The pottery', in Cromarty, A.M., Foreman, S. and Murray, P., The excavation of a late Iron Age enclosed settlement at Bicester Fields Farm, Bicester, Oxon. *Oxoniensia* 64, for 1999: 182-95.

Brown, K., 2001 'The later prehistoric, Roman and later pottery', in Cook, S. and Hayden, C., 'Prehistoric and Roman settlement near Heyford Road, Steeple Aston, Oxfordshire.' *Oxoniensia* 65, for 2000: 179-84.

Brown, L., 2000 'The pottery', in Cunliffe and Poole 2000: 53-84.

Bryant, S., 1994 'From Chiefdom to Kingdom', in Branigan, K. (ed.), *The Archaeology of the Chilterns from the Ice Age to the Norman Conquest*, Sheffield: 49-66.

Burl, A., 1991 *Prehistoric Henges.* Shire Archaeology 66, Princes Risborough.

Büttner, W., 1998 "Umb besser frides, Nutzes und schirmes willen". *Archäologie in Deutschland* 1998.1: 49.

Caes., *B. Gall.* = Caesar, *Bellum Gallicum.*

Castle, S.A., 1975 'Excavations in Pear Wood, Brockley Hill, Middlesex, 1948-1973.' *Transactions of the London and Middlesex Archaeological Society* 26: 267-77.

Chambers, R.A., 1993 'The Archaeology of the M40 through Buckinghamshire, Northamptonshire and Oxfordshire, 1988-91.' *Oxoniensia* 57, for 1992: 43-54.

Charles-Edwards, T.M., 1976 'Boundaries in Irish Law', in Sawyer, P.H. (ed.), *Medieval Settlement*, London: 83-7.

Christensen, L., 2003 'Olgerdiget.' *Reallexikon der Germanischen Altertumskunde*, 2nd edn, 22, Berlin and New York: 91-2.

Clarke, G., 1979 *The Roman Cemetery at Lankhills.* Winchester Studies 3.ii, Oxford.

Copeland, T., 1989 'The North Oxfordshire Grim's Ditch: A Fieldwork Survey.' *Oxoniensia* 53, for 1988: 277-92.

Copeland, T., 2002 *Iron Age and Roman Wychwood*, Charlbury.

Coy, J.P., 1987 'Animal bones', in Fasham 1987: 45-53.

Crawford, G., 1982 'Excavations at Wasperton: 2nd interim report.' *West Midlands Archaeology* 25: 30-44.

Crawford, O.G.S., 1930 'Grim's Ditch in Wychwood, Oxon.' *Antiquity* 4: 303-15.

Crawford, O.G.S., 1931 'The Chiltern Grim's Ditches.' *Antiquity* 5: 161-71.

Creighton, J., 2000 *Coins and Power in Late Iron Age Britain*, Cambridge.

Croom, A.T., 2001 'The Iron-Age Finds', in Hodgson, N., Stobbs, G.C. and Van der Veen, M., An Iron-Age Settlement and Remains of Earlier Prehistoric Date beneath South Shields Roman Fort, Tyne and Wear. *The Archaeological Journal* 158: 141-6.

Crow, J.G., 1986 'The Function of Hadrian's Wall and the Comparative Evidence of Late Roman Long Walls', in *Studien zu den Militärgrenzen Roms III. 13. internationaler Limeskongreß, Aalen 1983*. Forschungen und Berichte zur Vor- und Frühgeschichte in Baden-Württemberg 20, Stuttgart: 724-9.

Cunliffe, B., 1981 'Money and society in pre-Roman Britain', in Cunliffe, B. (ed.), *Coinage and society in Britain and Gaul: some current problems*. CBA Research Report 38, London: 29-39.

Cunliffe, B., 1984 *Danebury: an Iron Age hillfort in Hampshire 2. The excavations 1969-1978: the finds*. CBA Research Report 52, London.

Cunliffe, B., 1991 *Iron Age Communities in Britain*, 3rd edn, London and New York.

Cunliffe, B., 1993 *Wessex to A.D. 1000*, London and New York.

Cunliffe, B., 2005 *Iron Age Communities in Britain*, 4th edn, London and New York.

Cunliffe, B. and Poole, C., 2000 *The Danebury Environs Programme. The Prehistory of a Wessex Landscape 2.5. Nettlebank Copse, Wherwell, Hants, 1993*, English Heritage and Committee for Archaeology Monograph 49, Oxford.

Curtis, N., 1994 *The Ridgeway*, 2nd edn, London.

Darling, P.J., 1984 *Archaeology and History in Southern Nigeria. The ancient linear earthworks of Benin and Ishan* i. BAR Int. Ser. 215(i), Oxford.

Darling, P.J., 1997 'Sungbo's Eredo: Africa's largest monument.' *Nigerian Field* 62.3-4: 113-29.

Darling, P.J., 1998 'Aerial Archaeology in Africa: the challenge of a Continent.' *AARGnews* 17: 9-18.

Darvill, T., Stamper, P. and Timby, J., 2002 *England. An Oxford Archaeological Guide from Earliest Times to AD 1600*, Oxford.

Davis, R., 1797 *A New Map of the County of Oxford*.

De Jersey, P., 2001 'Cunobelin's Silver.' *Britannia* 32: 1-44.

Denison, S., 1999 'Parish boundary that may date from the Bronze Age.' *British Archaeology* 49: 4.

Diod. Sic. = Diodorus Siculus.

Domesday Book 14, Oxfordshire: Morris, J. (ed.), 1978, Chichester.

Dyer, J.F., 1961 'Dray's Ditch, Bedfordshire, and Early Iron Age Territorial Boundaries in the Eastern Chilterns.' *The Antiquaries Journal* 41: 32-43.

Dyer, J.F., 1963 'The Chiltern Grim's Ditch.' *Antiquity* 37: 46-9.

Erwin, P., 1999a 'Archäomagnetismus.' *Archäologie in Deutschland* 1999.2: 60.

Erwin, P., 1999b 'Middleton Stoney/ Upper Heyford, Archaeomagnetic dating at Aves Ditch (SP 5185 2465).' *South Midlands Archaeology (CBA South Midlands Group)* 29: 69.

Esmonde Cleary, S., 2000 'Putting the dead in their place: burial location in Roman Britain', in Pearce, J., Millett, M. and Struck, M. (eds), *Burial, Society and Context in the Roman World*, Oxford: 127-42.

Evans, J., and Booth, P., 2002 'Iron Age pottery', in Booth *et al.* 2002: 270-5.

Eyrbyggja Saga: Quinn, J. (transl.), 2003 'The Saga of the People of Eyri', in *Gisli Sursson's Saga and The Saga of the People of Eyri* with introd. and notes by Ólason, V., London.

Fasham, P. J., 1987 *A 'Banjo' Enclosure in Micheldever Wood, Hampshire (MARC3 Site R27)*. Hampshire Field Club and Archaeological Series Monograph 5, Gloucester.

Ferguson, J., 1978 'China and Rome.' *Aufstieg und Niedergang der Römischen Welt* II, 9.2, Berlin and New York: 581-603.

Field, J., 1993 *A History of English Field-Names*, London and New York.

Fine, D., 1977 'An Excavation of the North Oxfordshire Grim's Ditch at North Leigh.' *Oxoniensia* 41, for 1976: 12-16.

Ford, S., 1981-82 'Linear earthworks on the Berkshire Downs.' *Berkshire Archaeological Journal* 71: 1-20.

Ford, S., 1983 'Fieldwork and Excavation on the Berkshire Grims Ditch.' *Oxoniensia* 47: 13-36.

Fox, Sir C., 1955 *Offa's Dyke*, London.

Gelling, M., 1953 *The Place-Names of Oxfordshire* I, Cambridge.

Gelling, M., 1979 *The Early Charters of the Thames Valley*, Leicester.

Glob, P.V., 1969 *The Bog People. Iron-Age Man Preserved*, London.

Gosden, C. and Lock, G., 1998 'Prehistoric histories', in Bradley and Williams 1998: 2-12.

Grant, A., 1975 'The animal bones', in Cunliffe, B., *Excavations at Portchester Castle 1: Roman*, London: 378-408.

Grant, A., 1982 'The use of toothwear as a guide to the age of domestic ungulates', in Wilson, B., Grigson, C. and Payne, S. (eds), *Ageing and Sexing Animal Bone from Archaeological Sites*. BAR Brit. Ser. 109, Oxford: 91-108.

Grant, A., 1984 'Animal husbandry', in Cunliffe 1984: 496-548.

Gregory, T.E., 1993 *The Hexamilion and the Fortress*. Isthmia V, Athens and Princeton.

Grettir's Saga: Fox, D. and Pálsson, H. (transl.), 1975 *Grettir's Saga*, Toronto and Buffalo (cf. Jónsson, G., 1936 *Grettis Saga Ásmundarsonar*, Reykjavík).

Griffiths, B., 1996 *Aspects of Anglo-Saxon Magic*, Hockwold-cum-Wilton.

Grundy, G.B., c. 1933a *Ancient Highways of Oxfordshire*.

Grundy, G.B., 1933b *Saxon Oxfordshire. Charters and Ancient Highways*. Oxfordshire Record Series 15, Oxford.

Gsell, S., 1920a *Histoire Ancienne de l'Afrique du Nord* II, Paris.

Gsell, S., 1920b *Histoire Ancienne de l'Afrique du Nord* III, Paris.

Haberland, W., 1991 *Amerikanische Archäologie*, Darmstadt.

Halliday, R., 1997 'Criminal graves and rural crossroads.' *British Archaeology* 25: 6.

Hands, A.R., 1998 *The Romano-British Roadside Settlement at Wilcote, Oxfordshire II. Excavations 1993-96*. BAR Brit. Ser. 265, Oxford.

Harden, D.B., 1937 'Excavations on Grim's Dyke, North Oxfordshire.' *Oxoniensia* 2: 74-92.

Harden, D.B., 1939 'Romano-British Remains B. Roads', in Salzman 1939: 271-81.

Harding, D.W., 1972 *The Iron Age in the Upper Thames Basin*, Oxford.

Harding, D.W., 1974 *The Iron Age in Lowland Britain*, London and Boston.

Hargreaves, G.H., Parker, R.P.F. and Boarder, A.W.F., 1974 'Aves Ditch.' *CBA Group 9 Newsletter* 4: 10-11.

Harman, M., Molleson, T.I. and Price, J.L., 1981 'Burials, bodies and beheadings in Romano-British and Anglo-Saxon cemeteries.' *Bulletin of the British Museum (Natural History)* 35: 145-88.

Hawkes, C.F.C. and Crummy, P., 1995 *Camulodunum 2*. Colchester Archaeological Report 11, Colchester.

Hawkes, J.W., 1987 'The Pottery', in Fasham 1987: 24-39.

Heimberg, U., 1981 *Gewürze, Weihrauch, Seide: Welthandel in der Antike*. Kleine Schriften zur Kenntnis der römischen Besetzungsgeschichte Südwestdeutschlands 27, Stuttgart and Aalen.

Heimbs, G., 1925 'Der Angrivarierwall bei Leese a.d. Weser.' *Praehistorische Zeitschrift* 16: 59-64.

Henig, M. and Booth, P., 2000 *Roman Oxfordshire*, Stroud.

Herodian.

Herodotus.

Hill, D. and Worthington, M., 2003 *Offa's Dyke. History & Guide*, Stroud.

Hinchliffe, J. with Robinson, M., 1976 'Excavations at Grim's Ditch, Mongewell, 1974.' *Oxoniensia* 40, for 1975: 122-35.

Hodder, I., 1977 'Some New Directions in the Spatial Analysis of Archaeological Data at the Regional Scale (Macro)', in Clarke, D.L. (ed.), *Spatial Archaeology*, London, New York and San Francisco: 223-351.

Huff, D., 1981 'Zur Datierung des Alexanderwalls.' *Iranica Antiqua* 16: 125-39.

Humphrey, J. with Claxton, J. (eds), 2003 *Re-searching the Iron Age*. Leicester Archaeology Monographs 11, Leicester.

Iscan, M.Y., Loth, S.R. and Wright, R.K., 1984 'Age estimation from the ribs by phase analysis in males.' *Journal of Forensic Sciences* 29: 1094-104.

Jacobs, J. with Macfarlane, A., Harrison, S. and Herle, A., 1990 *The Nagas. Hill Peoples of Northeast India. Society, Culture and the Colonial Encounter*, Stuttgart.

James, S., 2003 'Writing the Legions: The Development and Future of Roman Military Studies in Britain.' *The Archaeological Journal* 159, for 2002: 1-58.

Jankuhn, H., 1976 'Befestigungen und Befestigungswesen § 5. Langwälle.' *Reallexikon der Germanischen Altertumskunde*, 2nd edn, 2, Berlin and New York: 141-2.

Jankuhn, H., 1985 'Grenzbefestigungen zwischen germanischen Stämmen in der älteren römischen Kaiserzeit', in *Lebendige Altertumswissenschaft. Festgabe zur Vollendung des 70. Lebensjahres von Hermann Vetters*, Vienna: 260-1, pls XXXII-XXXIII figs 1-3.

Jewell, P.A. (ed.), 1963 *The Experimental Earthwork on Overton Down, Wiltshire 1960*, London.

Jones, B. and Mattingly, D., 1990 *An Atlas of Roman Britain*, Oxford.

Karl, R., 2004 'Celtoscepticism: a convenient excuse for ignoring non-archaeological evidence?' in Sauer 2004a: 185-99.

Kennett, W., 1695 *Parochial Antiquities Attempted in the History of Ambrosden, Burcester and Other Adjacent Parts In the Counties of Oxford and Bucks*, Oxford.

Kent, J.T., Briden, J.C. and Mardia, K.V., 1983 'Linear and planar structure in ordered multivariate data as applied to progressive demagnetization of palaeomagnetic remanence.' *Geophysical Journal of the Royal Astronomical Society* 75: 593-621.

Keyser, R., 1854 *Religion of the Northmen*, New York.

Kiani, M.Y., 1982 *Parthian Sites in Hyrcania. The Gurgan Plain*. Archäologische Mitteilungen aus Iran Ergänzungsband 9, Berlin.

Killick, R.G., 1984 'Northern Akkad project: excavations at Habl As-Sahr.' *Iraq* 46: 125-9, pl. VIII.

Knight, S., 2003 'The importance of being processed: butchery patterns from Danebury', in Humphrey 2003: 25-34.

Kolník, T., 1999 'Gab es einen Limes Quadorum? – Langwälle in der Südwestslowakei', in Fischer, T., Precht, G. and Tejral, J. (eds), *Germanen beiderseits des spätantiken Limes*, Cologne and Brno: 163-77.

Lambrick, G., 1998 'Frontier territory along the Thames.' *British Archaeology* 33: 12-13.

Lancel, S., 1995 *Carthage. A History*, Oxford and Cambridge, Mass.

Laxdœla Saga: Magnusson, M. and Pálsson, H. (transl.), 1975 *Laxdœla Saga*, London.

Lobel, M.D. (ed.), 1959 *The Victoria History of the Counties of England. A History of the County of Oxford VI. Ploughley Hundred*, Oxford.

Lucy, S. and Reynolds, A. (eds), 2002 *Burial in Early Medieval England and Wales*. Society for Medieval Archaeology Monograph 17, London.

MacDonald, J.L., 1979 'Religion', in Clarke 1979: 404-33.

Magilton, J., 2003 'The Defences of Roman Chichester', in Wilson, P. (ed.), *The Archaeology of Roman Towns. Studies in honour of John S. Wacher*, Oxford: 156-67.

Maltby, M., 1981 'Iron Age, Romano-British and Anglo-Saxon animal husbandry', in Jones, M. and Dimbleby, G., (eds), *The Environment of Man*. BAR Brit. Ser. 87, Oxford: 155-94.

Margary, I.D. 1973 *Roman Roads in Britain*, 3rd edn: Trowbridge.

Meaney, A., 1964 *A Gazetteer of Early Anglo-Saxon Burial Sites*, London.

Meaney, A.L., 1984-1985 'Ælfric and Idolatry'. *Journal of Religious History* 13: 119-35.

Metzler, J., 1995 *Das treverische Oppidum auf dem Titelberg* 2, Luxembourg.

Mildenberger, G., 1978 *Germanische Burgen*, Münster.

Miles, D., 1986 'The Iron Age', in Briggs, G., Cook, J. and Rowley, T. (eds), *The Archaeology of the Oxford Region*, Oxford: 49-57.

Miles, D., 1998 'The Tom Hassall Lecture for 1996. Conflict and Complexity: The Later Prehistory of the Oxford Region.' *Oxoniensia* 62, for 1997: 1-19.

Miles, D., Palmer, S., Lock, G., Gosden, C. and Cromarty, A.M., 2003 *Uffington White Horse and Its Landscape: Investigations at White Horse Hill, Uffington, 1989-95, and Tower Hill, Ashbury, 1993-4*. Thames Valley Landscapes Monographs 18, Oxford.

Millett, M., 1990 *The Romanization of Britain*, Cambridge.

Morley Davies, A., 1947-52 'The Hundreds of Buckinghamshire and Oxfordshire.' *Records of Buckinghamshire* 15: 231-49.

Morse, R., 1995 'Fritwell, East Street (SP 5281 2948).' *South Midlands Archaeology* 25: 52.

Moxham, R., 2001 *The Great Hedge of India*, London.

Musgrave Archive 4 = Ashmolean Museum, University of Oxford, online resource: http://www.ashmolean.museum/php/am-makepage.php?&db=musgrave&view=list&filet=&arcno=&peop=&subj=&titl=&plac=&obj=&strt=&what=Search&s1=filetitle&s2=mainid&s3=itemtitle&dno=25&cpos=4

Napoli, J., 1997 *Recherches sur les fortifications linéaires Romaines*. Collection de l'École Française de Rome 229, Paris and Rome.

Neumann, H., 1982 *Olgerdiget – et bidrag til Danmarks tidligste historie*, Haderslev.

Noel, M. and Batt, C.M., 1990 'A method for correcting geographically separated remanence directions for the purpose of archaeomagnetic dating.' *Geophysical Journal International* 102: 753-6.

O'Brien, E., 1999 *Post-Roman Britain to Anglo-Saxon England: Burial Practices Reviewed*. BAR Brit. Ser. 289, Oxford.

O'Neil, B.H.S., 1929 'Akeman Street and the River Cherwell.' *The Antiquaries Journal* 9: 30-4.

O'Neil, B.H.S., 1944 'The Silchester Region in the 5th and 6th centuries A.D.' *Antiquity* 18: 113-22.

Ó Ríordáin, S.P. (rev. by De Valera, R.), 1979 *Antiquities of the Irish Countryside*, London and New York.

OSD 1814 = *Ordnance Surveyors' Drawings* 223, Ser. 182, 2", 1814.

Paret, O., 1932 *Die Römer in Württemberg 3: Die Siedlungen*, Stuttgart.

Pearce, J., 1999 'The Dispersed Dead: preliminary observations on burial and settlement space in rural Roman Britain', in Baker, P., Forcey, C., Jundi, S. and Witcher, R. (eds), *TRAC 98, Proceedings of the Eighth Annual Theoretical Roman Archaeology Conference*, Oxford: 151-62.

Peddie, J., 1987 *Invasion: The Roman invasion of Britain in the year AD 43 and the events leading to their occupation of the West Country*, Gloucester.

Penn, W.S., 1961 'Springhead: temples III and IV.' *Archaeologia Cantiana* 74, for 1960: 113-40.

Penn, W.S., 1965 'Springhead: the temple ditch site.' *Archaeologia Cantiana* 79, for 1964: 170-89.

Philpott, R., 1991 *Burial Practices in Roman Britain. A survey of grave treatment and furnishing A.D. 43-410*. BAR Brit. Ser. 219, Oxford.

Pinkerton, J. (rev. by Metcalfe, W.M.), 1889 *Pinkerton's Lives of the Scottish Saints* I, Paisly.

Pitt-Rivers, A., 1892 *Excavations in Bokerly and Wansdyke, Dorset and Wilts. with observations on the human remains* III, London.

Pitts, M., Bayliss, A., McKinley, J., Boylston, A., Budd, P., Evans, J., Chenery, C., Reynolds, A. and Semple, S., 2002 'An Anglo-Saxon Decapitation and Burial at Stonehenge.' *Wiltshire Studies* 95: 131-46.

Pl., *Leg.* = Plato, *Leges.*

Planck, D., 1982 'Ein neuer römischer Limes in Württemberg.' *Archäologische Ausgrabungen in Baden-Württemberg* 1982: 94-9.

Plot, R., 1677 *The Natural History of Oxford-Shire, Being an Essay toward* [sic] *the Natural History of England*, Oxford.

Pöll, J., 2002 'Spuren alter Verkehrswege in Nordtirol – Geleisestraßen', in Schnekenburger, G. (ed.), *Über die Alpen: Menschen, Wege, Waren*, Stuttgart: 73-81.

Pope, J.C. (ed.), 1967 *Homilies of Ælfric. A Supplementary Collection* I. Early English Text Society 259, Oxford.

Pope, J.C. (ed.), 1968 *Homilies of Ælfric. A Supplementary Collection* II. Early English Text Society 260, Oxford.

Potts, W. 1907 'Ancient Earthworks', in Page, W. (ed.), *The Victoria History of the County of Oxford* II: 303-49.

Procopius, *Goth.* = Procopius, *De bello Gothico.*

Procopius, *Pers.* = Procopius, *De bello Persico.*

Raddatz, K., 1981 'Die römische Kaiserzeit im mittleren Niedersachsen', in *Führer zu vor- und frühgeschichtlichen Denkmälern 48. Hannover • Nienburg • Hildesheim • Alfeld I: Einführende Aufsätze*, Mainz: 113-34.

Rahtz, P., Hirst, S. and Wright, S.M., 2000 *Cannington Cemetery.* Britannia Monograph 17, London.

Rahtz, S. and Rowley, T. 1984 *Middleton Stoney. Excavation and Survey in a North Oxfordshire Parish 1970-1982*, Oxford.

Rakhmanov, S.A., 1994 'The Wall between Bactria and Sogd: the study on the Iron Gates, Uzbekistan', in Kozintsev, A.G., Masson, V.M., Solovyova, N.F. and Zuyev, V.Y. (eds), *New Archaeological Discoveries in Asiatic Russia and Central Asia.* Archaeological Studies 16, Sankt-Petersburg: 75-8.

Ralegh Radford, C.A., 1936 'The Roman Villa at Ditchley, Oxon.' *Oxoniensia* 1: 24-69.

Ray, K., 1991 'South Oxfordshire District (SU 6965 8588 (centre)) Swan Wood. Highmoor.' *South Midlands Archaeology* 21: 80-1 with fig. 1.

Rebuffat, R., 1984 'Propugnacula.' *Latomus* 43.1: 3-26.

Rees-Jones, J. and Tite, M., 2003a 'Optically Stimulated Luminescence Dating', in Miles *et al.* 2003: 75-8.

Rees-Jones, J. and Tite, M., 2003b 'Optically Stimulated Luminescence (OSL) Dating Results from the White Horse and Linear Ditch', in Miles *et al.* 2003: 269-71.

Reynolds, A., 1997 'The Definition and Ideology of Anglo-Saxon Execution Sites and Cemeteries', in De Boe, G. and Verhaeghe, F. (eds), *Death and Burial in Medieval Europe* 2, Zellik: 33-41.

Reynolds, A., 1998 'Executions and hard Anglo-Saxon justice.' *British Archaeology* 31: 8-9.

Reynolds, A., 2002 'Burials, Boundaries and Charters in Anglo-Saxon England: A Reassessment', in Lucy and Reynolds 2002: 171-94.

Richards, J.D., 2000 'Cottam: An Anglian and Anglo-Scandinavian settlement on the Yorkshire Wolds.' *The Archaeological Journal* 156, for 1999: 1-111.

Rivet, A.L.F., 1958 *Town and Country in Roman Britain*, London.

Roberts, A., 2005 'Forgotten Records of Oxfordshire's Past.' *The Ashmolean* 48: 20-2.

Robinson, M.A. and Lambrick, G.H., 1984 'Holocene alluviation and hydrology in the upper Thames basin.' *Nature* 308: 809-14.

Salter, H.E. (ed.), 1908 *Eynsham Cartulary II.* Oxford Historical Society 51, Oxford.

Salway, P., 1981 *Roman Britain*, Oxford.

Salzman, L.F. (ed.), 1939 *The Victoria History of the County of Oxford* I, Oxford.

Samuel (Old Testament).

Šašel, J. and Petru, P. with Leben, F., Matejčič, R. and Urleb, M., 1971 *Claustra Alpium Iuliarum*, Ljubljana.

Sauer, E., 1998 'Middleton Stoney/ Upper Heyford, Aves Ditch, an Iron Age linear earthwork (SP 51852465).' *South Midlands Archaeology (CBA South Midlands Group)* 28: 73-5.

Sauer, E., 1999a 'Alchester (Oxfordshire) 1998: new fieldwork reveals Roman fort and an early road.' *Bulletin of the Association for Roman Archaeology* 7: 4-6.

Sauer, E., 1999b 'Aves Ditch: an Iron Age Tribal Boundary?' *Current Archaeology* 163: 268-9.

Sauer, E., 1999c 'Erdwerk und Römerlager in Oxfordshire.' *Archäologie in Deutschland* 1999.2: 56-60; cf. 1999.3: 57.

Sauer, E., 1999d 'Middleton Stoney/ Upper Heyford, Aves Ditch, earthwork and tribal boundary of the Iron Age (SP 5185 2465/ SP 5195 2481).' *South Midlands Archaeology (CBA South Midlands Group)* 29: 65-9.

Sauer, E. with contr. by Crutchley, S. and Erwin, P., 1999e 'The Military Origins of the Roman Town of Alchester, Oxfordshire.' *Britannia* 30: 289-97, pl. XXIV.

Sauer, E. with contr. by Cooper, N.J., Dannell, G.B., Dickinson, B., Erwin, P., Grant, A., Henig, M., McDonald, A.W. and Robinson, M., 2001 'Alchester, a Claudian 'vexillation fortress' near the western boundary of the Catuvellauni, new light on the Roman invasion of Britain.' *The Archaeological Journal* 157, for 2000: 1-78.

Sauer, E., 2002 'The Roman invasion of Britain (AD 43) in imperial perspective: a response to Frere and Fulford.' *Oxford Journal of Archaeology* 21.4: 333-63.

Sauer, E. (ed.), 2004a *Archaeology and Ancient History: breaking down the boundaries*, London and New York.

Sauer, E., 2004b 'Introduction', in Sauer 2004a: 3-16.

Sauer, E., 2004c 'Wendlebury (Alchester fortress): the 2003 season (SP 570 203).' *South Midlands Archaeology (CBA South Midlands Group)* 34: 78-84.

Sauer, E., 2005 'Inscriptions from Alchester: Vespasian's Base of the Second Augustan Legion(?)' *Britannia* 36: 101-33.

Saunders, T.J., 1991 *Plato's Penal Code: Tradition, Controversy, and Reform in Greek Penology*, Oxford.

Schlüter, W., 1999 'Zum Stand der archäologischen Erforschung der Kalkrieser-Niewedder Senke', in Schlüter, W. and Wiegels, R. (eds), *Rom, Germanien und Kalkriese. Internationaler Kongress der Universität Osnabrück und des Landschaftsverbandes Osnabrücker Land e.V. vom 2. bis 5. September 1996*. Osnabrücker Forschungen zu Altertum und Antike-Rezeption 1, Osnabrück: 13-60.

Schottky, M., 1998 'Quellen zur Geschichte von Media Atropatene und Hyrkanien in parthischer Zeit', in Wiesehöfer, J. (ed.), *Das Partherreich und seine Zeugnisse*. Historia Einzelschriften 122, Stuttgart: 435-72.

Schuchhardt, C., 1900 'Römisch-Germanische Forschungen in Nordwest-Deutschland.' *Neue Jahrbücher für das Klassische Altertum, Geschichte und Deutsche Literatur* 3: 90-116.

Schuchhardt, C., 1931 *Die Römer als Nachahmer im Landwehr- und Lagerbau*. Sitzungsberichte der preussischen Akademie der Wissenschaften, phil.-hist. Klasse 23, Berlin.

Schumer, B., 1999 *Wychwood. The evolution of a wooded landscape*, Charlbury.

Sellwood, L., 1984a 'Objects of iron', in Cunliffe 1984: 346-71.

Sellwood, L., 1984b 'Tribal Boundaries Viewed from the Perspective of Numismatic Evidence', in Cunliffe, B. and Miles, D. (eds), *Aspects of the Iron Age in Central Southern Britain*. University of Oxford: Committee for Archaeology Monograph 2, Oxford: 191-204.

Semple, S., 1998 'A fear of the past: the place of the prehistoric burial mound in the ideology of middle and later Anglo-Saxon England', in Bradley and Williams 1998: 109-26.

Sherwood, J. and Pevsner, N., 1974 *The Buildings of England: Oxfordshire*, Harmondsworth.

Silver, I., 1969 'The ageing of domestic animals', in Brothwell, D. and Higgs E. (eds), *Science in Archaeology*, London: 293-302.

Simek, R., 1984 *Lexikon der germanischen Mythologie*, Stuttgart.

Simmer, A., 1982 'Le prélèvement des crânes dans l'Est de la France à l'époque mérovingienne.' *Archéologie Médiévale* 12, 1982: 35-49.

Sleeman, W.H. (Smith, V.A. [ed.]), 1893 *Rambles and Recollections of an Indian Official*, new edn, II, London.

Soproni, S., 1985 *Die letzten Jahrzehnte des Pannonischen Limes*. Müncher Beiträge zur Vor- und Frühgeschichte 38, Munich.

Spratt, D.A., 1982 'The Late Bronze Age', in Spratt, D.A. (ed.), *Prehistoric and Roman Archaeology of North-East Yorkshire*. BAR Brit. Ser. 104, Oxford: 167-84.

Spratt, D.A., 1989 *Linear Earthworks of the Tabular Hills, Northeast Yorkshire*, Sheffield.

Stark, J., 1988 *Haithabu – Schleswig – Danewerk. Aspekte einer Forschungsgeschichte mittelalterlicher Anlagen in Schleswig-Holstein*. BAR Int. Ser. 432, Oxford.

Steuer, H., 1999. 'Grenze § 2. Archäologisches.' *Reallexikon der Germanischen Altertumskunde*, 2nd edn, 13, Berlin and New York: 5-10.

Stork, I., 1995 'Ausgrabungen im fränkischen Friedhof und der frühmittelalterlichen Siedlung in Kirchheim am Neckar, Kreis Ludwigsburg.' *Archäologische Ausgrabungen in Baden-Württemberg*, for 1994: 232-5.

Suchey, J.M. and Brooks, S., 1990 'Skeletal age determination based on the os pubis.' *Human Evolution* 5: 227-38.

Sutton, J.E.G., 1968 'Iron Age Hill-Forts and some other Earthworks in Oxfordshire.' *Oxoniensia* 31, for 1966: 28-42.

Tac., *Ann.* = Tacitus, *Annales*.

Tac., *Hist.* = Tacitus, *Historiae*.

Tallon, P., 1999 'What was a Caldecote?' *Journal of the English Place-Name Society* 31, 1998-1999: 31-54.

Thomas, J., 2003 'Prehistoric pit alignments and their significance in the archaeological landscape', in Humphrey 2003: 79-86.

Thomas, N., 1958 'Excavations at Callow Hill, Glympton and Stonesfield, Oxon.' *Oxoniensia* 22, for 1957: 11-53.

Thompson, I., 1982 *Grog-tempered 'Belgic' pottery of South-eastern England*. BAR Brit. Ser. 108, Oxford.

Thompson, V., 2002 'Constructing Salvation: A Homiletic and Penitential Context for Late Anglo-Saxon Burial Practice', in Lucy and Reynolds 2002: 229-40.

Thurlow Leeds, E., 1939 'Anglo-Saxon Remains', in Salzmann 1939: 346-72.

Trotter, M. and Gleser, G.C., 1958 'A re-evaluation of estimation based on measurements of stature taken during life and of long bones after death.' *American Journal of Physical Anthropology* 16: 79-123.

Ulbert, T., 1981 *Ad Pirum (Hrušica)*. Müncher Beiträge zur Vor- und Frühgeschichte 31, Munich.

Vaday, A., 2002 'Militia inermis, militia armata: Bemerkungen zur Frage des Limes Sarmatiae.' *Slovenská Archeológia* 49, for 2001: 249-76.

Van Arsdell, R.D., 1989 *Celtic Coinage of Britain*, London.

Van Arsdell, R.D. with De Jersey, P., 1994 *The Coinage of the Dobunni. Money Supply and Coin Circulation in Dobunnic Territory*. University of Oxford: Committee for Archaeology Monograph 2, Oxford.

Von den Driesch, A. and Boessneck, J., 1974 'Kritische Anmerkungen zur Widerristhöhenberechnung aus Längenmaßen vor- und frühgeschichtlicher Tierknochen.' *Säugtierkundliche Mitteilungen* 22: 325-48.

Von Petrikovits, H., 1967 'Über die Herkunft der Annäherungshindernisse an den römischen Militärgrenzen', in *Studien zu den Militärgrenzen Roms. Vorträge des 6. internationalen Limeskongresses in Süddeutschland*, Cologne and Graz: 215-20.

Wacher, J., 1995 *The Towns of Roman Britain*, 2nd edn, London, New York, Sydney and Toronto.

Waddell, J., 1998 *The Prehistoric Archaeology of Ireland*, Galway.

Waldron, A., 1990 *The Great Wall of China: From History to Myth*, Cambridge.

Warton, T., 1783 *Specimen of a History of Oxfordshire. Kiddington*, 2nd edn, London. [The information on Aves Ditch in the 1st and 3rd edn is similar.]

Watt, R.J., 1979 'Evidence for decapitation', in Clarke 1979: 342-4.

Whittaker, C.R., 1994 *Frontiers of the Roman Empire*, Baltimore and London.

Wilkinson, T.J., 2003 *Archaeological Landscapes of the Near East*, Tucson.

Williams, H., 1997 'Ancient Landscapes and the Dead: The Reuse of Prehistoric and Roman Monuments as Early Anglo-Saxon Burial Sites.' *Medieval Archaeology* 41: 1-32.

Wilson, D., 1992 *Anglo-Saxon Paganism*, London and New York.

Wilson, D.R., 1975 'Roman Britain in 1974. Oxfordshire (2) Roman roads, Fritwell.' *Britannia* 6: 256-7.

Winchester, A., 2000 *Discovering Parish Boundaries*, 2nd edn, Princes Risborough.

Woodward, A., and Marley, J., 2001 'The Iron Age pottery', in Ellis, P. Hughes, G. and Jones, L., 'An Iron Age boundary and settlement features at Slade Farm, Bicester, Oxfordshire: a report on excavations, 1996.' *Oxoniensia* 65, for 2000: 233-48.

Woolliscroft, D.J., 2001 *Roman Military Signalling*, Stroud.

Workshop of European Anthropologists 1980 'Recommendations for age and sex diagnoses of skeletons.' *Journal of Human Evolution* 9: 517-49.